For the Love of Horse

By Lynn Hummer

Print ISBN: 978-1-54396-647-3
eBook ISBN: 978-1-54396-648-0

TO MY HUSBAND, DAVE. THANK YOU FOR A LIFETIME OF LOVE, SUPPORT, FRIENDSHIP AND BELIEVING IN ALL MY CRAZY DREAMS...EVERY SINGLE ONE OF THEM.

I'll travel to the new unknown, expectedly become vulnerable, and ask my physical self to be silent. I will call upon my spirit and heart. Your spirit, or heart side is where the breaking down of boundaries begins. Love and understanding live there.

LYNN HUMMER

The greatness of a nation can be judged by
the way its animals are treated.

MAHATMA GANDHI

TABLE OF CONTENTS

CHAPTER 1

The Crazy Horse Lady

Soaking up the sun and overlooking the harbor is a delightful way to spend a Friday afternoon. The tink-tink sound of the shrouds or cables clinking against the sailboat masts in the breeze made music with the squawking seagulls. Seaside afternoons were crisp and welcoming. I was lifting a refreshing glass of chilled chardonnay to my lips. The chatter of the crowd around me was telltale that folks were busy celebrating an ended week of work. I wasn't trying to eavesdrop when a voice behind me caught my attention.

"They poop when you let them."

Well, I knew instantly what they were discussing. God knows our dogs drag us all over the neighborhood peeing and squatting as they please. We carry plastic bags around tidying up after them like indentured servants. Cats would likely fall off their fence boards in laughter at the notion of being so controlled, but not our beloved horses. They serve, love and take what we hand out in complete silence.

My husband, Dave, shot me a look as if to inquire, "Where are you?"

I mentally snapped back to our table and the guests in front of me. I smiled and reluctantly refocused my attention on the conversation at hand, but I wasn't successful. My mind began to wander.

Why do people control horses like that? I pondered the question. In all my years spending time in the company of these magnificent creatures, I have witnessed unnecessary control and unfortunately a lot of brutality on the part of humans. Once again, that little nagging voice popped in my head. It's the voice I have been trying to ignore for many years. The voice was demanding once again for me to recognize that the time had come for me to ask the enormous question. Why? Why are horses treated so poorly in every corner of the world?

Outright equine abuse is obvious and prevalent in many cultures. One would hope the majority of horse-loving people would find these actions cruel and brutal, but these actions either directly (*by being an incident to view*) or indirectly (*by being an abusive method to create a desired effect*) provide entertainment for some people and make money for others. Thus, these many practices have become entrenched in many cultures, still exist, and, unfortunately, are very widely accepted.

The hard part when confronting these abusive actions is that many cultures view themselves as exempt from doing better, because that's the way "it's always been." It doesn't seem to make a difference that the general opinion outside the culture is that it is no more than abuse. So the horse loses in every culture and on every playing field. Those in competition call it "sport" and the abuses have been well documented for years. Other activities are deeply ingrained and regarded as cultural events.

We can look at what is deemed "blatant abuse." For example, Mexican-style rodeos, Charreadas, are a national sport in its home country and are host to several cruel and barbaric events. Of 10 different competitions, six of them are horrifically abusive to horses. One such event is titled "horse tripping." Points are awarded for literally tripping horses by running them, lassoing their legs and tripping, in which they crash to the ground. Those that survive the first round are sent back through again and again—until death.

Another illustration of blatant abuse is found on the other side of the world in Europe. Originating in Germany, Rollkur has been deemed extremely abusive. This practice in equestrianism defined as "flexion of the horse's neck achieved through aggressive force" is banned by the world governing body, the International Federation for Equestrian Sports (FEI). The problem is it is still occurring. It's been 12 years since international public outrage of this abusive training technique began gaining traction in 2006, but the FEI continues to ignore the tens of thousands of equestrians who have protested the use of Rollkur. I have seen photos of horses in head harnesses that enforce this position for hours.

How must that feel for a horse? Close your eyes and imagine standing against a wall. Now slide down the wall with your back vertical and your thighs bearing the weight of your body. How long can you do it? How long before your legs scream in pain and then you begin to cramp. You can't move to escape the burning…next comes panic. Would you lose your mind? This is Rollkur for a horse.

Another instance of blatant horse abuse occurs in the world of Tennessee Walking Horses. "Soring" involves the intentional infliction of pain to a horse's legs or hooves in order to force the horse to perform an artificial, exaggerated gait. Caustic chemicals—blistering agents like mustard oil, diesel fuel and kerosene—are applied to the horse's limbs, causing extreme pain and suffering. A particularly egregious form of soring, known as pressure shoeing, involves cutting a horse's hoof almost to the quick and tightly nailing on a shoe, or standing a horse for hours with the sensitive part of his soles on a block. This causes excruciating pressure and pain whenever the horse puts weight on the hoof. In the arena, when the Tennessee Walking horse is made to move, the horrid look that is desired is called The Big Lick. Sad? Yes. Disgusting? Now you can understand why the nagging voice in my head won't go away.

But my focus and bigger concern starts with the people who are not part of these titled barbaric practices. They are the everyday horse folk that believe in their heart that they are doing right by their horses. These are the horse people that think they are not abusing their horses in any way. Yet, I believe they are. The horses are suffering in silence right under the eyes of all humanity. These people partake in subtle, yet damaging choices that, in my opinion, keep the magical partnership from ever happening and keep the abuse alive and well—all to the detriment of the horse they claim to love. I would like to shed light on their accepted choices for handling their horses—their beloved horses. If this information can be shared and understanding can happen then maybe, just maybe, the world for horses will improve.

Many years ago I thought that there were lots of different methodologies that work well for training horses. I wasn't suggesting one way as the only way. But as I watched and learned, studying the really great trainers in action, I had to reconsider my statement. There is only one way to achieve remarkable results when working with horses, and that is with relationship and trust training. Each respected trainer working with the horse had developed the ability to create trust and understanding, and then went on to see amazing results.

I state this clearly and confidently because horses when given the chance are more than willing companions. Think about that for a moment. If the horse is not a willing companion, it is the responsibility of the horse handler to figure out and examine why.

Why is this true? Because horses are honest by nature and being honest is all they know. They don't lie, manipulate, create agendas, or become difficult for the fun of it. They live in the moment, each moment, every day of their lives. If there is a problem, it is simply never the horse's fault.

I also witness that all disciplines of riding can be done without ever intimidating, coercing or abusing the horse. Yes, you read that correctly. The disciplines of dressage, English equitation, jumping, western roping, barrel racing, reining and cutting, trail riding, and even, of course, some horse racing. I have witnessed partnerships in each of these disciplines where horse and rider are one. There is no abuse present.

Of course, as one can imagine, it is not easy to accomplish this level of expertise! It takes longer, and in some cases much longer, because you're approaching "training" with a completely new mindset. This mindset is one of building trust and creating relationships. It's about giving the horse the chance to understand. Trainers refer to it as "setting the horse up for success." Without this mindset, everything else a trainer does is only promoting his or her own agenda. It can be as simple as a timeframe to be met, but it is still the person's agenda, not the horses.

A great read addressing the very topic of keeping your training on the horse's agenda is the book *Gallop to Freedom*, written by Magali Delgado and Frederic Pignon. In 2003, the remarkable talents of these two were brought to the stage in a never-before-seen live production "Cavalia." The spectacular, equestrian-themed extravaganza demonstrated the powerful connection they have developed with their beautiful horses. The relationship demonstrated so much more than "training." This beautifully choreographed event was a mesmerizing dance between horse and human, and the show contained lots of riding, not just poetic on-the-ground movements. We can all learn from these experts.

In the past decade, the miracles I have witnessed between horse and human have convinced me of my truth. The good news is there is a movement out in the world of horses and it's gaining recognition. Horse folks are beginning to see the light. Trainers of every background and discipline are all beginning to see there is a gentler, more effective way to do things when working with horses, and it's no surprise the results are phenomenal. The not-so-good news is that it's taking time.

Wouldn't every horse person choose kinder methodologies if the result produced happier, healthier horses and better partnerships? There is a bigger picture looming and I call it the human agenda. The human agenda will always get in the way of what I believe to be fair, honest, just and better-made partnerships. It's my title for all the decisions and actions humans make while living on this planet Earth. A human being's desire for wealth, status, or convenience are the motivations driving the destruction of natural habitats, and the abuse or obliteration of animal populations all over the globe. The sustainability of our world and the animal populations we share it with remain threatened and a safe future for them remains bleak. Whether or not you believe in global warming doesn't matter. These are facts, plain unarguable statistics, which shed light on a very real tragedy. I have read humans are referred to as a parasite on the planet Earth. It's much bigger than the world of horses. But for now we are speaking about horses.

"Hey," the quiet, patient husband murmured. "What will you order?"

Jolted back once again to my company, I smiled and metaphorically stepped down off my soapbox. Choosing my entrée I heard the voice again. I was annoyed, as such expertise, such authority, came bellowing from behind me.

"If she is that difficult for you, maybe it's time for a change! Maybe you should get rid of her?"

Ugh, it was all I could take! Get rid of her? Don't we get rid of poison oak, smelly shoes and old food? If I were a smoker I would have had to go outside for a cigarette. I had visions of chucking my chardonnay over my right shoulder. I wanted to stand up and turn around and say in my best smart-ass tone of voice, "Oh Pardon me, I didn't realize you were taking up space behind me, sucking up usable air. Sit up straight in your chair! No, you cannot use the rest room! Now, read the menu and wait your turn to order! Maybe we should get rid of you?"

Well, I don't smoke, and I happen to have lovely manners, so I just glared at my husband who has seen the familiar frustrated look before.

"You ok?" he asked.

"Trying," I responded.

It takes a crazy passion, or perhaps a crazy person, to begin the task of changing the mind of a nation. I hope to be the former but I think I may indeed be the latter. In any case, it's a long road to understanding that the way many horses have been treated for years isn't the way they need to be treated at all. A long road I am paving with my love, sweat, and hell-bent intention.

I invite you to come and discover what I believe to be the true nature of horses. I would like to share with you the ups and downs of dreaming about effecting change, creating and living horse rescue. Along the journey we will examine horse intelligence, their capacity to forgive and, most importantly, their role as healers. I will share some of my personal stories as my life becomes so entwined with my rescues that I can't imagine getting through a crisis without them! If you're ready to follow along in the many adventures of horse rescue, you better keep in mind that it is not easy, nor is it fair. It is not a paying gig, and the rescues don't always appreciate the intervention…at least not at first anyway. Come along and see for yourself that the time for a new approach has arrived. I believe in my heart of hearts that the good in people can be brought forth, and that fostering understanding can indeed effect change. I choose to believe that each one of us can glean something from this writing and do better by our horses. The time to recognize the horse has arrived and the time to protect them from abuse is now.

CHAPTER 2

Crafting My Thoughts About Abuse

I n all my years of trading sweat and labor for riding privileges, I had never owned my very own horse. Observing horse owners for years had left me with lingering doubts about exactly how I would be able to achieve the connection I knew I wanted. It appeared solid and attainable with the horse whisperers, the people who make it their craft to understand equines. Could I have the same experience? I knew it was what I desired.

In my daily observations, the equestrians I encountered were fairly rude, often egotistical and the horses all appeared miserable. I would walk the barns at dusk and see the vacant eyes: horse after horse standing in a box. Horses are herd animals and it is etched in their DNA to be part of a group and to move. I viewed that isolation, created as a convenience for the rider, to be a death sentence for an equine. I wasn't sure how all my thoughts and inclinations would play out, but as my mind began to churn, I created a very well organized idea about the kind of relationship/partnership for which I was yearning.

From 1990 to 2005 my family and I were living in Campbell, California in a cute little cottage type track home, complete with window boxes and a white picket fence. With children tucked in, I sat up late nights surfing the internet learning all I could about the current lives of horses, specifically what happens to horses over the course of their lifetime, and what happens to them when they are no longer wanted by their current owner. I learned that a horses' very life could be dependent upon its usefulness. A horse that cannot be ridden may well be euthanized, abandoned or even shot. Less than 1 percent of American horses have only one owner during their lifetime. I also learned that the majority of horse owners would euthanize (kill) their horse if it cannot be ridden. It is widely accepted and considered the kinder action to take, rather than sending them to slaughter. Horses are expensive to keep, and if one cannot enjoy their horse for the intended purpose, which is to be ridden, then they kill them so that they may go purchase another. It probably would become disturbing to people if you remove the word horse and replace with dog or cat …if they become less than playful or not as great a companion in say their later years do you kill them? Do you turn them in and get a younger model? (Horrifically some people do!)

This was initially shocking to me. How naïve could I possible be? I had witnessed that a large portion of horse people employ practices in their daily routines that display impatience with our equines, and now, I discovered, that for a myriad of reasons they discard them at whim without a second thought. I found this astonishing. I was under the impression that little girls all over the world were being taught to treat their equine mounts with love and respect. I thought the old time ranchers retired their horses out to pasture after their years of hard work. Maybe some do, but I felt now I had discovered I might be wrong.

With a little more digging—and a lot more thought—I decided I would just begin with the definition of words. This would perhaps

help me see the broader perspective from a human point of view…
the general opinion if you will.

> **Horse:** a solid-hoofed, plant-eating domesticated
> mammal with a flowing mane and tail, used for rid-
> ing, racing, and to carry and pull loads.
>
> I observe the words used for, and *to carry and pull*.
> I did not see pet. I also didn't see any reference to
> being companion, sentient being, best friend, ther-
> apist or other.
>
> **Equine:** a horse or other member of the horse family.
>
> **Livestock:** Broadly, livestock refers to any breed or
> population of animal kept by humans for a useful,
> commercial purpose.
>
> **Stock:** A supply of something for use or sale.

Well, that explains a lot right there. The definition a lot of
humans still live by is outdated, antiquated, and not really useful
any longer. It's like thinking there is only one mouse. A mouse is
not just a small rodent that typically has a pointed snout, relatively
large ears and eyes, and a long tail. While the definition of a mouse
held its place alone at the top in the dictionary for a very long time,
things have now changed. It is now also a tool to move a cursor on
a computer screen. It's time to step into the present day and recognize the horses are more than "livestock."

An unimaginable disregard for life was my best understanding of such a heinous process as simply discarding or getting rid
of your horse. It has now been well documented that horses are
brilliant companions, and they are healers. Honest and true, they
serve, love and even protect us. I had assumed all these years that
horse people, those people who love and spend time in the company of horses, treated them wonderfully. Again, I began to see my
presumptions had been very wrong.

I watched a beautiful lengthy documentary on Icelandic horses. Of course, they are from Iceland and their breed is now fiercely protected. They are extremely regulated, and the breed remains pure. It was stated no other breed existed on the island and they consider these horses, their horses, to be an extremely superb equine. They have two extra gaits making riding a pleasure, they are extremely hardy in the cold climate and have a very amicable disposition. Imagine my horror when the gentleman interviewed, a hardy Icelandic horseman, made mocking reference to "this romantic idea" of letting horses live out their days in pasture, as if they deserved anything for being such devoted servants. His horses were spoken about and referred to as commodities, like products. He belittled the idea that a horse may have a heart and feelings. This dumbfounded me. You name them, breed them, ride them, have them help earn your living and sustain your family, and then…well, then slaughter them and throw them in your freezer? I had to question how one could spend a lifetime in their company and never be touched by their gifts, or ever realize their value beyond "livestock."

The time to act was upon me. That nagging voice finally won. I was compelled to learn all I could about how this worldwide attitude, this horrible apathetic attitude toward horses, came to be. I held out a small lingering hope that they simply did not know any better. But, in my heart, I had a feeling this was not the case.

CHAPTER 3

A Life Changing Lesson

My daughter Jillian, at the age of 10, was my horse companion and best buddy. Five times a week we would make the trek up to our local stables, a mere 45 minutes away to muck stalls and scoop grain in exchange for horse time. The moments and afternoons spent in the company of the horses were full of laughter and sweaty hugs. Only one of us could ride as we only had one horse, but we both worked on the stall, the dinner and, of course, taking care of the horse.

Concho was a lovely quarter horse gelding with a calm mind and very sweet soul. He patiently waited for his treats and rewarded us with soft rocking horse canters on warm summer evenings. Often we just strolled around the grounds sharing our own experiences of time with this amazing boy. It was a world away from school and life pressures and it was filled with outdoor fragrances of horse and wildflower aromatherapy. I was such a country girl at heart—always yearning for the space of the great outdoors and the chance to meet wildlife face to face. I could see so much of myself in this little girl of mine. The more open space, the better.

It was one weekend at the end of spring that I pulled Jillian out of school early Friday for a surprise. We were going on a "little jaunt." The expression and anticipation on the face of my little fifth-grader was priceless.

She questioned, "Does it involve horses?"

"Well, of course," I chuckled. "How'd you guess?"

I was interested in seeing just how sanctuaried horses lived. What were the wild horses really like? Were they really so much different than domesticated horses?

We packed and repacked and made sure all was in order. I tucked her into bed along with her excitement knowing we'd be up before the sun, as we'd be heading out at about 4 a.m.

Right on schedule the sun peeked up above the horizon and welcomed a new morning as we trekked up Interstate 5. It's a long, straight and seemingly endless highway that runs right down the middle of California from north to south. It was in predictable fashion this morning. No accidents or delays but it seemed, as it did every time one drove it, to go on for forever! We enjoyed our coffee and hot chocolate as we made our way north. Sitting low in the sky at about 8:30 am the sun provided streaming rays as we pulled into the driveway.

A few rocky crunches underneath the tires and we had arrived at The Wild Horse Sanctuary. I noticed an old white fence peeled and warped from years of baking sun. It would guide us into our spot for parking. An enormous oak generously provided some shade. There were no clouds in the sky and heading to this part of Northern California this time of year meant it could be a warm day. There would be no Bay Area fog to keep the temperature low. Lake Shasta is a gorgeous area in Northern California and springtime is filled with green rolling hills and wildflowers making their brief appearance before the summer heat descends.

At the ranch we were introduced to a group of folks that would be accompanying us for the next 24 hours on our journey. The plan was to ride all day across some 2,000 acres, enjoy the wild horses and burros in their natural habitat and spend the night at base-camp. My understanding was that a warm shower, a hot meal, a glass of wine, and primitive digs awaited us. I glanced at the crowd and took comfort seeing so many different aged people waiting and ready for the adventure. Jillian was the youngest in the group, and I would soon see she was also the most comfortable rider. We said hello to our horses and thanked them for indulging us for the trip. Carrots made a good first impression.

We handed our bags over to a couple of ranch hands, made a quick restroom break, and mounted. Jillian and I were on our way, anticipating the large expanse of rolling landscape and numerous bands of wild horses to be seen. Lots of dried leaves and prickly brush rolled about on the ground. I glanced to see the ground squirrels racing for protection into their big holes as the ranch gate closed behind us. We were on our way.

Instructions were shared as we began out on the open plain. Never position yourself between a mare and her foal. Never approach the stallion. There will be one stallion in each group. The rest are mares and the mares are his harem. It is his job to pro-tect his harem, so ride with the pack and keep a calm energy. No screaming, whooping or big loud gestures. We are guests in their home, so let's act like it.

We dutifully walked about an hour single-file, keeping our excitement under wraps. The morning air smelled of dirt and horses. Perfect. We came upon an odd little structure. It had three crooked sides draped in cobwebs. While it resembled a barn I wasn't sure if it was standing or this was it in its fallen down state. It was a sad little structure at best. As we rounded to the open side there stood a pair of little burros. The sun highlighted the dust floating in the air as it was gleaming thru the wooden board cracks. Fairy dust danced in and out of the light, and bounced off their black noses. The burros tucked a bit closer to one another and as we strolled past I noticed their long ears moving and bending, following us as we plodded along.

"These girls are from the Nevada range and the Bureau of Land Management (BLM). They were rounded up and brought to us to live here in sanctuary. All the horses you will encounter on this trip are wild." Dianne Nelson, the founder, went on to explain, "Back in 1978, rather than allowing 80 wild horses living on public land to be destroyed, we made a major life decision right then and there to rescue these unwanted horses and create a safe home for them."

She added, "We saw the need to create an alternative to the slaughtering of these animals."

Wait, what? My head spun around and glanced at her silhouette. Sitting in the saddle with the brim of her hat shading her eyes, she quietly began to speak again. I moved my mount up a little closer to better hear her words.

This moment, this pause in breathing and the profound realization of what her words were telling…this experience changed my life. I was frozen in thought. They slaughter horses in America? This was 2005. Were they still slaughtering American horses? Other countries I knew all about, but America?

"…To inspire others to also be a voice for America's wild horses."

She finished her short narrative and we began to walk on. A long stretch of path ended as we rounded a small knoll to an area of rolling oaks. Most of the grass was brown with lots of mature trees, their branches slung low to the earth, throwing long areas of shade. More dust swirled and settled. I thought about the burros, the girl's ages were unknown. They looked healthy. I was grateful they had each other in their little three-sided barn. They looked happy and content. They slaughter horses in America? I was still stunned.

Closer to the trees, I noticed horses tucked up next to the trunk. Tails swishing and heads low, it appeared as though there may be seven or eight mares.

Dianne calmly said, "Mares are shaded up. The stallion is probably near, let's be alert. Let's keep moving." Her leg was the only cue given to her horse. The reins lay over the saddle horn untouched, loose. I noticed they moved as one.

As we sauntered out of the grove of old oaks we began a small ascent. We all leaned forward helping our horses take on the new grade. The grass began to appear in little baby sprouts along the trail. We continued and the earth lost the cover of dust, becoming a darker soil as it was still covered in morning dew. Hooves left their mark. The moist earthy smell filled my nostrils. It was still early spring so the temperature was mild and welcoming.

By midday—just like an old Western movie—the sun was high in the sky. We dismounted and brought our horses to shade and water. As we chose a log, sat and settled, Dianne inquired if we were thirsty.

"Follow me here if you'd like some fresh water."

I hopped up curious as to where she might go. A little grassy bump hid a pulsating flow of water bubbling up onto the ground. She crouched over bended knees, cupped her hand and collected a mouthful. I was questioning...Giardia? Is it clean? Safe? Without allowing the question to be asked, she laughed, "I don't want any sick guests on my watch. Please, enjoy!"

I tried the cool, crisp, wet, wonderful water right out of the ground. I was amazed. Spring water was clean and satisfying. I threw some onto my face and cupped the back of my neck. Ah, heaven.

Dianne had positioned us at the site of a cave. We again were invited to explore. While I didn't venture in, I did experience the transition in temperature as I descended to the large opening. Each big boulder felt cool to the touch and with each step down the air became colder. I felt as if this must be what the animals experience everyday, as wildlife, this is their reality. The breezes swirled every now and then, but if you weren't paying attention you'd miss it. The temperature of the air from moment to moment shifted.

I found myself needing to stand and close my eyes. I wanted to take in each nuance. The little hairs on my arm stood up with the cool sensation. Jillian popped her head out of the cave entrance announcing she was going inside. I smiled and headed back up to the grass…one boulder at a time.

The group was resting in varied places around the cave. A couple clearly enamored and needing no one but each other for company was picnicking against a fallen log. Another group of women were chatting and sharing their thoughts about the morning. One young lady, about 17, was standing stroking her horses face; the quiet space the two of them held was a picture of peace.

With the lunch break ending, our instructions were to mount up and head for basecamp. The vast rolling plain ahead showed we had more riding hours to go. The grasses moved as the short-legged prairie dogs scurried about. On high alert, their chirping didn't end until we were out of site. Red-tailed hawks with enormous wing-spans screamed as the hunt above us continued. Were we interrupt-ing their task at hand? Circling and diving, they were stealth. Stoic and intense, they were focused on their meal.

A band of mares appeared and joined us as we walked along in a lazy fashion. Heads hung a bit low, kind of slow and easy, they plodded along as if they were content just to walk alongside a bit and check us out.

I glanced in Jillian's direction to catch her smiling. We were sharing a thought. How cool is this? We are walking with wild horses! The feeling of calm was comforting as the horses were all so at ease. There was a unified thought, an unspoken directive, as we all moved in unison. Well-worn saddles creaked and an occasional snort was all the noise made amongst the group. The smell of dust began to rise once again as we continued to mosey on. A creek bed divided us and we headed off in our own direction. I quietly bid farewell to the mares and watched as their tails swished and danced away.

We rode into basecamp by afternoon. The ranch hands helped us dismount and walk our horses over to the water. The stiffness felt in my legs quickly reminded me of my hours in the saddle. Done for the day, the horses were turned out onto an enormous fenced grassy pasture. I watched as my pal took a nice roll and big shake before starting to graze. I slipped him another carrot while I took in the view, appreciating the gorgeous landscapes in every direction.

By definition a "buck and rail" fence consists of two poles crossed in an "X" pattern and is connected to a series of poles running parallel to the ground and attached along one side. This fencing gives the feel of a time long past, including a gate that closed with only a board. I noted no concrete and no nails. This gave it the look of 100 years ago.

There were seven tiny cabins lined in a row with a wooden walkway that connected them all. Once inside I noticed I could see sunlight peeking through the space between boards and I noted it was simply a board—one thick board—between us and the great outdoors. I took in one window next to the door: two queen-sized mattresses on wooden frames, a nightstand and lantern. Simple, rustic, perfect. Our bags had been placed upon our beds. I smiled as I noticed our door closed with a board as well.

Outside, untouched grass easily four feet tall grew in between each hut. The main cabin in the center was the largest and would be occupied by our host. The kitchen was there and all the amenities a guest might request. It was the only structure with running water and electricity. Our shower was a claw-foot tub with a curtain decorated in spurs n' boots, and one plate-sized round showerhead directly above at about seven feet. It was like standing in warm rain.

As dusk arrived, the ranch folk threw out flakes of hay. It was distributed generously across the meadow right in front of the walkway. Far off the meadow was a pretty good-sized pond. A few mares had arrived and were drawing water, standing knee deep with lowered heads. Showered and fed, Jillian and I sat on the edge of the wooden walkway, our boots touching the grass. Our hosts were readying a bonfire. More of the mares began to arrive with their little foals trotting alongside, their long spindly legs trying to keep up. It was a very peaceful setting. The foals jousted and romped while the mares grazed.

Jillian stood and moved over toward a lone standing scrub oak. She rested against the trunk observing the magnificent horses, wild horses, so close! A mare the color of chocolate lifted her head and gazed at my daughter. As the breeze lifted her mane, her eyes blinked and she moved in her direction. It was a quiet effortless walk. It didn't feel angry or annoyed. Jillian didn't move and watched to see just what this would mare do. I held my breath. Looking around I saw no one was paying attention as they were beginning to gather around the fire. I wasn't sure of protocol. Should she move? Should she freeze or retreat? What would this mare do? How dangerous was this?

Before I could answer my own questions Jillian reached out her hand and placed it directly on the mare's neck. The connection was made, quiet and still. Neither moved. Oh shit? Is that okay to do? I mean I can't get to her if this mare strikes. But there would be no such action. As easily as she had approached, she retreated back to the herd. She stood quietly for moment looking over her shoulder back in Jillian's direction and then moved off. I exhaled quietly.

The last bit of sun was now low in the sky and the striking orange rays lit up the chest of the stallion about 50 yards out. An enormous wall of strength pounded onto the scene. Head lowered, ears pinned flat, snaking his way across the meadow and at an extended and aggressive trot. My heart lurched into my throat.

I yelled to Jillian, "Get up on the porch! Get back!"

I couldn't help but notice his dappled coat was the color of a brand new shiny penny. Dazzling, blazing…his muscles rippled against his frame. The mares lifted their heads acknowledging his presence. Foals took notice and quickly found their place against mom. This magnificent horse went straight for the chocolate mare.

What happened next can only be described as our National Geographic moment. He mounted her and then proceeded to mount every mare in his harem. He attended to the tree by urinating all around the base. When finished he took a moment to glance at the humans standing, observing in complete stunned silence. If a look of disgust is possible, it was coming from the stallion. I believe that's what we got. He was unimpressed and remained perturbed. He walked to the pond to drink. The mares resumed their relaxed posture and the foals began to once again romp and play in the grass. The remainder of the evening was uneventful. Well, what could top that? His territory had been claimed, his harem reminded of just who was in charge. We enjoyed the crackle of the fire and watched as the horses eventually disappeared into the darkness.

Morning found another reminder of strength and territory. Every inch of ground around our cabin was trampled. Nobody else's grass was touched. But ours was stomped to dirt. A good days ride must make for a great night's sleep. We never heard a sound. Our hosts commented, "It was Copper. He's a crabby ol' man." I chuckled to myself thinking, that's it? Well, these guys aren't big on words. I had a fleeting thought about all the fuss about sex education in schools, what's appropriate and what isn't, and the moral implications and arguments for and against. Out here it was so, well, part of nature, part of the landscape. Simply part of life.

And so this experience at the Wild Horse Sanctuary became my inspiration. This story began over 12 years ago all because of two blissful days completely connected to nature. I was part of the landscape, part of the breeze. I belonged whole-heartedly to the moment. Being. No doing, no agenda. Just being. I had never experienced such peace or such a connection to Mother Earth and all her inhabitants.

Now heading home, I knew I had to learn about horse slaughter in America. I had to learn about why people, after so many years, still don't get horses. I wanted to know why the abuse continued. A generalization cannot be made insulting or condemning any one culture, country or continent. I observe an extreme lack of understanding of what equines are capable of physically, spiritually, and emotionally by people all over the world. It simply exists everywhere. I conclude it is the condition of being human.

I mentioned early on my thoughts on the human agenda. Yes, dirty egotistical financial motivation is, unfortunately, alive and well. But what about good old folks who own horses and believe in their heart of hearts they are doing right by them?

My answer is they don't know any different and ego is blinding. This is a deadly combination and I mean for the horses. People have been taught a certain way to achieve desired results and that's what they do. It's all they know and changing a mind or habit is a pretty tough thing to do, even if one was instructed on how to do so. The financial implications play a big part, as does being lazy. Convenience kind of falls in with being lazy, but I believe EGO plays the biggest part in keeping horses misunderstood and abused.

Can you let go, for your horse, for the love of horse?

CHAPTER 4

Let's Just Test Drive This Baby

Now, I'm pretty sure you're saying to yourself, "I'm exempt, not me, I am good to my horse. I love, *love* my horse!" But your curiosity is aroused. I will leave it for you to decide just how well you treat your horse. So, let's read on.

I'd like to ask some simple straightforward questions. Depending on your response we can examine the consequence to the horse.

Question-A: You and your horse have been training for an "event." You both have time, energy, definitely money, emotion, and expectation invested. The morning of the event your horse is off. The horse could be sick, lethargic, looking lame, not cooperating. You know your horse well enough to know that something is up. How do you proceed?

1. Withdraw from the competition. Nothing is worth the risk of possibly putting your horse in harms way.

2. Get opinions from other horse people. Explain what you think is going on and then make a decision.

3. Get a vet opinion IF he can come before "showtime," otherwise back to option two.

4. Get a vet out to assess the horse before you do anything with him, even hauling him home.

5. Look to the vet to camouflage symptoms. Inject hocks, deliver pain killers, drugs…whatever it takes to compete.

If you chose answers one and/or four, then you respect your horse's wellbeing and are interested in keeping him safe and healthy. The rest of the choices are putting your agenda ahead of your horse's wellness. If you were vacillating and considering answer number two, let me remind you that horse people have more opinions and answers than Kleenex has tissues. Don't waste your energy there.

Question-B: You're entertaining at your ranch and your guests are thrilled to be around the horses. They are enjoying alcohol and want to ride.

1. You politely say no. Alcohol and horses don't mix, certainly when the horse doesn't know these people. You offer a rain check.

2. You are not sure how to say no, and feel maybe just walking around would be fine. You saddle the horse and let them ride.

3. You're having a blast and feel the horse will be fine. After all, the horse is in his own corral and you're there to watch over everyone.

4. You were not even aware your guests are hopping on bareback and whopping it up.

The horse is hoping you're going to choose number one. Alcohol and its effects are very noticeable to horses. It frightens them, thus, making their fear response heightened. Even my horses will respond differently to me if I have had one glass of wine in the evening. They are sensitive and live in the moment. It is incredibly unfair to the horse, not to mention dangerous, to do anything else.

Jean Luc Cornille wrote in detail about the horse's fine-tuned senses in his 2018 essay, "From the Horse's Mouth: Look out for my Umwelt."

We can hear what you cannot hear. We can smell what you cannot smell but because in your Umwelt, (Each species evolves the Umwelt which allows it to extract from the external world the information its ancestors needed to survive) your sight is your main perceptual tool, you look in the direction we are looking at and you judge us in respect of what you see or don't see. Sorry to burst your bubble but having your excellent visual perception as your main tool of perception limits you to what you can see. At night, or for long distance, the sight is limited; the smell is not. Instead of convincing yourself that there is nothing, you should believe us. There is a wolf or a hare that you cannot see. A terrible thing happened there weeks or more ago and we can smell it. When you are afraid of us, or you are angry because your day did not go well, your body secretes molecules that we can smell. You can draw a smile on your face but we can smell behind your smile.

Trust me on this. If you have consumed alcohol, they know it.

Question-C: Mr. Biggs is usually very cooperative when it comes to loading into a trailer. But today the trailer being used is different than what he is accustomed to. He balks at the entrance and cements both feet on the ground outside the trailer. You are trying to get him to a scheduled appointment. What do you do?

1. Get out your dressage whip, carrot stick, or long stick, and start harassing him from behind.

2. Start clapping behind him to scare him and make him move.

3. Back him up and move him around and reintroduce him to the trailer.

4. Give him the opportunity to figure out that it is safe.

5. Start pulling on his neck making sure not to let go.

6. Smack him on the rump as hard as it takes.

7. Keep him focused on the trailer, pull and release with praise at the slightest effort he exhibits.

8. Keep your agenda out of it. It takes as long as it takes.

Your horse is hoping you'll take numbers three, four, seven and eight. He's hoping for a chance to feel safe.

So, how did you do? Hard isn't it? And those are only three scenarios of an unlimited amount of circumstances challenging you and how you treat your horse. Are you a great horse owner? It's extremely hard to make choices that always put the horse and its well being first. Agenda and timelines are huge obstacles. It takes great patience to do it right. Perhaps this exercise demonstrated just a hint of how small adjustments from you could indeed keep your horse well loved and safe.

So, I was back in Campbell in my cute little picket-fenced house. I began to research what was going on with America's horses and why they are at such risk? My very first horse was not my personal horse; she was a horse I rescued. Rose and I met, online. My initial experience in rescue was what I imagined an online dating site to be. Except that instead of finding a date, you were finding a life to save. Page after page, site after site, there were images and short biographies of every kind of horse imaginable. The time began to tick as they were dropped off, each lot giving about a week before the horses not "saved' would ship.

This was initially overwhelming to me. How many horses could be shipping to Canada and Mexico to slaughterhouses? My research would determine that easily more than 150,000 American equines ship to slaughter annually. They are not all old, crippled or broken, as the tales told would have you believe. It is because life changes and life happens. There are many reasons why horses end up on lots. In rescue, the lots are commonly referred to as "kill lots." The reason for this straightforward term is that the general public is led to believe they can bring their horse here to find them a new home. The reality paints a much darker picture. Very few horses sold here are rehomed to families or private parties. It's mostly men known as "kill buyers" that bid and buy up these horses. They haul them to Canada and Mexico to be slaughtered and make a very tidy profit. For the horse, this is a trip to hell with the destination titled death. Their meat is then shipped overseas for human consumption.

At this time I must address a two-pointed argument I hear daily. That *"horse slaughter is a necessary evil, and it is more humane to slaughter them here in the states as the U.S. the industry is better regulated and one eliminates the horrific journey."*

I will disprove both these notions, as horse slaughter is never necessary, ever. The solution to ending the unwanted overpopulation of horses is very simple. STOP breeding. Humans can (and should) be made responsible for the number of horses they put on the ground. Backyard breeders often tell me they want to make cash on their non-rideable mare, and big production barns with fancy horses of *every* breed are just as guilty. It's all about money. The circumstance surrounding our wild mustangs is filled with misleading propaganda centered on making the public believe our horse populations are soaring. This again is rooted in the desire for money.

We can create licensing, fees, registration, laws, and the accountability to regulate these activities. Cities, counties and states in our nation have all created these processes for dogs and cats. We do not need to reinvent the wheel here. It's not that hard and most certainly not impossible. However, greed combined with irresponsibility is great and, when you add convenience, it is lethal.

If you are thinking the horses going to the lots are old, crippled, or have something wrong with them, then your attitude is outdated. I share this as an example to make my point: Annually big breeding barns will impregnate say, 15 mares. A year later when the mares have all presumably foaled the new young lives are evaluated. The best eight or nine are kept and the less desirable foals are sent to slaughter—their dams along with them as they produced a less than perfect foal. There is nothing wrong with these horses unless you are seeking perfection. They are the product of human greed and the desire to create the best horse. I have taken a Thoroughbred mare and her colt and rehomed both of them successfully. Their conformation was not perfect, but their dispositions more than made up for the imperfection. They are well loved and never deserved to be at risk of a trip to the slaughterhouse.

The thought that slaughterhouses are better regulated in the U.S. is a misguided conclusion. This statement brings to mind an article written by Bill Bowden, published March 18, 2012 in the *Northwest Arkansas Democrat-Gazette*. That year, Paula Bacon was the mayor of Kaufman, Texas:

Bacon sent an open letter to U.S. legislators in September outlining the problems she said Kaufman encountered. Bacon wrote that the plant frequently overloaded the city's wastewater treatment facility, that the odor was offensive, and that leaky trucks hauled hides and offal through city streets.

City documents noted, "blood flowing" in ditches near the plant, Bacon wrote, (Sue) Wallis (former Wyoming representative and slaughter house advocate) told the crowd in Mountain Grove that the only issue with blood in a ditch in Kaufman occurred after a blood truck malfunctioned, spilling some blood. "It was cleaned up in two hours," she said. Wallis said people also heard false tales about horse blood coming up into showers and toilets in Kaufman. (Bowden, 2012)

False story? I ask who would make up a story like that? This is just one of many articles printed making statements about these plants reopening in the United States. Public outcry will be huge, and the general consensus against the slaughtering of our horses remains very high. I can never forget the story shared by a dear friend, Joan, a fellow woman in rescue.

It was now dark at the "auction" lot and the majority of folks had long headed home. Many horses had been loaded and on were on their way to new beginnings. A woman stood at the outdoor corral clearly keeping a beautiful chestnut horse company. She would talk and stroke his nose reassuring him all was well. Minutes ticked by and she just stood waiting. It was late so Joan approached her and asked if she could be of help. She explained that she was waiting to meet the new owners of her beloved boy. She had items that would go with him and she was anxious to share all his nuances. He was a wonderful well-trained boy. She further explained that a family medical emergency had left her no choice but a big life change. She wiped away the tears and shared that sometimes choice is not an option.

With tears of her own, Joan explained to her that all the remaining horses here now had not been the ones purchased by families. They had been scooped up by "kill buyers" and would be shipping out to Canada on Tuesday. It felt as the final blow had landed and the woman sank to her knees. She was reduced to sobs of hopelessness.

"Come," said Joan, "let's go buy your horse back."

This defeated soul began to protest explaining that she could not bring her boy home. Joan lifted the heap of sadness and walked her to the office. Once in the administration office, the sale was undone and the horse relinquished back to the two of them.

Walking to the paddock, Joan explained, "I rescue horses just like your boy. I try and come and save as many lives a week as I can. I will take him, and care for him and find him a home he deserves."

The trailer had room as Joan only had enough money to rescue one horse that evening. Her little two-horse trailer left full. Joan expressed that the feeling of being there to help—to be able to make a difference in someone's time of unbearable sorrow—is a life-changing experience. We understand so well that slaughter is not the answer.

In the past five or six years, the business of sending horses to slaughter has become even more difficult to navigate through and extremely controversial. Feedlot owners can be greedy business folks. They have learned that people sympathetic to horse abuse and neglect will pay a pretty price to "save a life." Lot owners have learned to pull the ugly, old, and sick ones and place them out back, far and away from bidders. These lives never ever have a chance to be saved. The healthier, pregnant, good-looking horses are then placed as "going to auction." Terms used are those like "shipping Tuesday, headed for the truck." You get it. The hysteria begins and the Internet lights up. Horses need saving. The crowd rallies and many horses are saved, while their price often times has been quadrupled. The lot owners move into the second round of their scam and announce they're going to do the public and these poor horses a favor and extend their shipping date by a week if needed. These particular horses will never see the slaughter plant or the truck. They have successfully made the lot owners a tidy profit, and they will all go into homes. It is the horses no one ever sees that lose.

They quietly ship out to their horrific destiny. Lot owners all over the nation are laughing all the way to the bank.

It has been noted time and time again that 80 percent of Americans oppose our horses going to slaughter. It is the general attitude from both sides of the political divide. Why can't a ban happen then? Why doesn't the atrocity stop? What's the problem? It would seem both sides agree, and most Americans concur, that we don't want our horses going to slaughter. So what is the problem keeping the laws from changing in this nation? Don't be surprised that it's money. It is politicians and the money they get, the promises they make, the favors they owe…That is the answer to the question of why this goes on and on.

And I would be remiss not to mention at this time that EVERY president has failed on his promises to safeguard the American mustang and American domestic horses from abuse and /or extinction.

CHAPTER 5

Rose Is My First

I f horsemeat is being calculated at 35 cents per pound, my first rescue cost me a little more than $300. Rose was our first and, as I have mentioned, we met online. I had scrambled and collected my dollars together and one night, immersed in that blue glow from my computer, I took the leap. I clicked my "send" button. Within moments I was the owner of my first horse. I stared at her picture. I had one picture—one link—of this little life on the edge. Each morning and every evening before bed, I would glance at that little image and think *just a few more days until I meet Rose*. I chose Rose because she was pregnant. I felt that, if possible, it would be good to give a baby a chance at life while saving the mom. She was small too, not too big for a beginning rescuer. She would be loaded at the Fallon, Nevada lot and hauled directly to me. No quarantine, just a health certificate to cross the border into California.

I will begin by saying I have never laid eyes on such a frightened creature in my whole life. I have seen quiet and withdrawn but I had never witnessed an animal in fear for its very life. She was trembling and hesitant, wincing as if a blow to her face may be coming at any second. I escorted her off the trailer and noticed her hooves as long as pair of Arabian slippers, turning up at the toe. I was thinking how bad hoof care puts a tremendous strain on horses' legs and then I noticed her belly. She was definitely pregnant. Between her baby weight and the terrible condition of her hooves, I knew she was in a lot of discomfort. She was quiet and so scared.

I kept whispering reassuringly, "It's ok now, I've got you."

The barn owner approached and my instructions were handed out in a matter-of-fact tone. I glanced around as I was shown the location of what was to be Rose's new home, well at least until Dave and I could buy our own dirt. The pasture was lovely and quite large, with a nice structure for protection standing sturdy and inviting. It was then I noticed something strange. It was an extremely large head, gazing out from under a barn fence board and this face was looking directly into my eyes. Chewing quietly and otherwise completely motionless, the large brown eyes watched and waited. I could see then that the red and white animal was a – cow? Do you mean to tell me my sweet, scared, pregnant young mare is going to take up residence with a cow? Will this work? I had to think a moment…what on earth do I know about cows?

"Hi Cow," I muttered. "Nice to meet you. This is Rose and she is going to be um…your new roommate. You good with that?" Cow blinked and continued to observe. Non-committal I thought. Okay…one step at a time.

Perhaps the look on my face revealed that the cow had caught me a bit off guard. Miss H., the owner of the facility, interrupted my meeting and stated confidently that cows and horses are fine.

She added, " I can tell by how you handle this horse, you are not sure of what you are doing." Huh? I had already gained her trust and helped this trembling life off the trailer. I was feeling competent and proud.

"I feel pretty good about what I'm doing," I responded pleasantly.

"Well, clearly this is your first horse experience!"

I just looked at her. What would possess someone to be so opinionated? Did my very presence threaten her? I'm the least threatening person I know. Could my lack of cow knowledge transfer over to a lack of horse knowledge? I'm sure my eyebrows were raised a bit, but I preferred not to make a fuss. Ignoring her comment, I chose to turn my attention to the guidelines at hand. Miss. H had lots of rules and they were expressed very clearly, long before Rose had even arrived. No rope halters, as they are deemed dangerous. No veterinarians or farriers allowed on the property without explicit permission from Miss H., and absolutely no trainers allowed on the property…period. I was prepared to be a good boarder and follow the rules.

I have to admit that I was disappointed nobody else seemed to be excited that my first little rescue had made it to us safe and sound. The passersby strolled on, no smiles, and without so much as a nod. I was bursting with pride at this lovely and round little mare. Couldn't they see how brave she was? It took all she had to trust that another blow to the head wasn't forthcoming. Her eyes were already showing relief, beginning to change, and becoming clear and soft. What a gorgeous little bundle of momma-to-be.

My smile wasn't contagious. The vet stood by looking on quietly. His job was to give her an examination and vaccinations. The examination revealed a very disabled little mare. Her walking was slow, tentative and shy. Her continued wincing became indicative of perhaps an injury or extreme discomfort. Beyond her bulging belly, her condition was poor: hooves too long, tendons strained, coat dull and shedding. This poor little mare was suffering.

"I heard you rescued this horse?" His glance in my direction was flat. "Why?" he inquired. "She apparently has sustained some sort of head injury. Her cognitive function is off, her mobility is limited, and by the size of her belly she appears in compromised health."

"Pregnancy is compromised health?" My inquiry was firm.

"She will never be of use," the vet retorted.

There was that word again.

"Can you define use?" My cheeks flushed.

I was feeling furious at the audacity of the vet making that kind of judgment on this horse. She was my horse and I was concerned about her wellbeing more each minute. It was clear that she was struggling yet I couldn't believe the vet had so chillingly dismissed this little life.

"Why would you bother," he asked.

"Because life matters, because I feel she des…" I was cut off before I had even answered.

The shot had been administered and he interrupted, "OK, I'm all done here, she can go to her stall." He walked away pocketing his pen.

Nice to meet you too, I thought. I felt like a 5-year-old child, wanting to stick my tongue out at him behind his back, maybe throw a rock at him. I walked slowly whispering to Rose, "Don't you worry. Old men can be very crabby. I am very proud of your bravery. You are a very important mare, and your baby is going to be perfect." I tucked her in, made certain she had fresh bedding hay and a full water trough. I headed home to learn about cows.

My daily visit had her nickering in no time. She'd lift her head in greeting.

"Hey Rose, how's it going today," I'd ask. She always replied, with another nicker from under her breath. My sister came out to meet the new edition to the family. I was appreciative of her excitement and looking forward to a nice visit. In less than a week's time, Rose had made tremendous progress settling. She seemed relieved and content all the while packing on the pounds. Our research revealed that Rose was a little quarter pony, barely 3 years old. She had been pulled off the auction yard by a horse rescue and was up for adoption.

My sisters continued enthusiasm was heart warming and welcome. The icy atmosphere of the barn was difficult at best and with baby on the way, I was disappointed with this initial experience.

"Can Carol come meet Rose?"

I smiled and scheduled a visit. Carol is Bravo's mom, a gorgeous gaited gelding. This means he is a beautiful neutered male horse (the gelding part) with wonderful movement when riding (the gaited piece). I have had the pleasure of riding Bravo and he is indeed a treasure. I knew Carol would fall in love with Rose just like Cathy and me.

"I said trainers are not allowed without explicit permission!"

I spun around to see who was caught in the wrath of Miss H. I couldn't believe my eyes when I found her glaring at me.

"What?"

The three of us stood still as though we had been caught doing something terribly wrong.

"Your trainer is not welcome here! You did not get permission!"

My mind clicked on and I realized the ridiculousness of her statement. Cathy and Carol shot questioning glances my way.

"Miss. H.," I began. "This is my sister I believe you have met, and Carol, our good friend."

"Well, we don't allow trainers on the grounds without permission," she persisted.

Now I was annoyed and felt the need to speak up. But older sisters have this unwritten rule. It states that when the little sister is being bullied, the big sister gets to step in, if she so chooses.

And choose she did. She began her inquiry very loudly.

"Did it occur to you that we are here to visit? Did it occur to you that Lynn's new horse is going to have a foal, and we are happy for her? This is not the first time you're presuming is incorrect."

You don't mess with my sister. I don't care who you are. She can and will chew you up and spit you out if she deems it necessary.

She continued, "Frankly your rudeness has made this whole experience unnecessarily difficult."

Cathy then turned her attention toward me and affirmed, "Lynn, I think we can find a better facility for Rose, before she foals."

Oh boy, OK, I thought, *that could work—I've only been here a few days but this can work.* My mind began to calculate pennies, number of days, hay, and hauling costs.

"I want 30 days notice paid in full." Miss H. turned in a huff and disappeared.

In a split second, my sister screamed. Carol and I spun 'round once again to see what could possibly have happened. Our roommate Cow has decided Cathy is his beauty and begins to put on his romantic advances. My sister had been knocked to the ground!

Oh shit.

"Cow!" I yelled. "Get away! Get away from her!"

Carol rushed in and began to pull Cathy back onto her feet. I stepped in front of the cow and grabbed his huge head. He swung it to the left and I went with it barely landing on my feet. The moment created our opportunity and we all scrambled out of the pasture in horror.

While the smell of horses has been romanticized and put into poetry, the smell of bovines has not, and Cow left us feeling smelly and gross. We brushed ourselves off, kissed Rose from the outside of the fence board, and made our way home. Only 10 days into our stay and it was definitely time for a new barn.

Morning number 11 arrived at the ranch and so did we—with our bolt cutters in hand. Animal Control of Santa Cruz County recommended I bring them along, just in case the unpredictable barn owner decided to play hardball. Until she had her additional 10 days of money in her hand, she may try, and held the right, to bolt the paddock. We punched in the gate key and rolled the rig up to the paddock gate. Gate key worked…*open says-a-me!* No bolt lock. Perfect. Cow stood at the far end of the pasture. Perfect.

The coast was clear and I went to work quickly pulling Rose out of the pasture. Remember Rose moves at less than a snail's pace and the term *quickly* should be taken with a grain of salt. We loaded up without incident and headed toward the exit gates. I tucked the additional 10 days board and my termination agreement into the mailbox.

We approached the exit and the wide gates began to pull back slowly. Freedom was so close! Hurry, hurry, I thought. Checking my rear view mirror I caught a glimpse of her flying out of the office. I could hear her yelling, "I'm calling the police. You owe me money!"

"Quick, quick go-go!!!" Our eyeballs were huge with anticipation as we lurched out onto the highway. I felt like we had just pulled off the great heist! Hitting the gas we lunged onto the payment, blowing up a cloud of dust behind us. Cathy turned back around to face frontwards and we began to laugh.

"Oh my God! Can you believe her! She's bat shit crazy!"

That was the last encounter I had with Miss H and I really wish I could say that this barn owner was a rare bird, but the honest truth must be told. Horse folk can be a breed unto themselves. Horse folks know this but, of course, that definition excludes them. Over the course of the next few years, I would come across more birds than I care to mention. Yes sir, some horse folk write their own reality.

For all the obvious reasons, which horse lovers understand, Rose became the center of our world. Daily trips back and forth to Santa Cruz kept us on the go. My daughter Jillian would grab a couple of friends and we'd head to the barn! We were elated just to get to use the phrase.

"Yes, we are on our way to the barn." The words felt sweet like candy rolling off the tongue.

"Our horse is going to have a baby." We quickly learned the correct usage of the language is in foal. "Our horse is in foal." We were feeling it and loving this new life!

One afternoon Jillian was caught exclaiming to her neighborhood chums, "This is horse hair, not dog hair. It's from our horse." All the little girls stood in silence. Their speechless faces, with raised eyebrows and little lips parted ever so slightly, were telltale of their envy. It was a dead giveaway. We were the new stars of the neighborhood.

My sister and her husband had stepped up to help baby proof Roses' new digs. It was a weekend filled with fixing gates and scrubbing water troughs. I lugged a bale of straw into the new paddock area and set it off to one side.

The woman who owned this barn was a much friendlier version than the previous barn owner. She was full of information; some useful, and well, some not so much.

She saw the new bale of straw on the ground and pronounced, "You're going to need to open that bale and spread the straw all around. Your horse is not going to go lay in one particular spot to have her foal."

No shit, Sherlock. I smiled and nodded.

"And your shoes are dangerous. Clogs are a big no-no out here." I crinkled my eyebrows and squinted. I have been wearing my Ariat clogs for a decade. I ride in them with my half-chaps. I muck stalls in them in the dry season. They are my seasoned, well-used testimonial that I am into horses!

"I think they are fine," I responded. I was polite but stood my ground.

"Well, I don't want to see them out here again. If you twist an ankle, you'll come sue me!" She turned and walked away never giving the subject, or me, I am quite certain, another thought. God what is it with barn managers, I thought to myself.

My daughter looked at me and giggled, "She's kind of a bitch huh?"

"Language please," was all I said. I hate correcting my children when they are spot on. It was getting late in the afternoon and time to leave, tummies would be grumbling.

We rolled into the driveway at dusk, smelly and tired. I picked up the ringing telephone, "Hello, this is Lynn."

"Your baby is on the ground!"

"What? Are you kidding me? We just pulled in."

"You have a little boy! Come quick."

We all piled back into the van like a band of tired soldiers, each hanging onto the coattails of the one in front. Back over the hill we went. Forty-five minutes later, a small crowd greeted us in front of the stall. There he was! A jet-black spindly little fellow was staring back at the crowd.

I popped under the fence boards and gave Rose a hug. The familiar nicker was warm and welcoming.

"Congratulations," I whispered. "Well done."

I sat in the (spread out) straw and watched mom and baby. It was then I noticed a small detail. He was not a he, but a she. I suppose an umbilicus can be mistaken for a tiny penis even in the best of light.

"We have a little girl," I smiled. "She's a girl!"

Sitting in the fresh straw with a brand new foal is an experience in itself. By nature they are curious. They are also cute, soft, magical, and warm. What is not to enjoy? This little girl came over sniffing and checking me out.

"What are you?" I could see the question forming in her mind. She stepped close and tried to suckle on my cheek, then my nose. She worked her way down to my chin and I had to giggle.

She retreated as fast as an uncoordinated 2-hour-old foal could do! Mom was waiting and nudged her reassuringly. She peeked around from behind mom's shoulder. She was sizing me up. For me it doesn't get any better than this. Keep Disneyland and trips to Paris. I'll choose to sit in the straw with a newborn foal.

The oohing and aahing continued until there was no part of the day left. With baby nursing and sleeping, and with Rose resting, we packed up for the drive home. Looking in the rear view mirror, I saw sweaty heaps of children resting quietly. The miracle of birth laid its magic over my brood. The air was warm and the silence was full of love. I peeked as eyelids gave way to rest. Tangled children sleeping blissfully, tired from all of the joy and excitement of the day. This filled my heart. I thought to myself, *these are the experiences to remember.*

CHAPTER 6

Can We Really Do this? How Can We Not?

Working full time and raising children is a challenge in itself. My husband and I have enjoyed an extremely blissful partnership for more than 28 years. To say he is the love of my life is an understatement. Even still, bringing up the topic of relocating for my new project and creating a horse rescue is a daunting task. Part of me lingered over the thought, *how can I get him to buy into this crazy idea?*

A new morning over coffee and my thoughts would drift toward a softer sales pitch, "But sweetheart, it would be so good for the kids!" My triumphant, liberated self argued that I deserved equal say and this was something I wanted us to seriously consider!

Dave is a quiet man with a dry sense of humor. Sometimes when he doesn't want to engage, he just doesn't reply at all. I was prepared to do battle. I was going to be heard. With all the reasons, excuses, yearnings defined, rights addressed, spiritual guidance, and emotional wellbeing thrown into the mix, I presented my case. Certainly he must know we all want to be closer to Rose?

"You've been putting a lot of thought into this haven't you?" he said.

"Well, yes, I really want to do this. I really want you to be on board."

Admittedly, I was feeling sheepish, as it's no small task to uproot an entire family. He began to summarize as though he were thinking aloud.

"You want to sell the house, move the kids into new schools, move the four of us in with your brother into his 900-square-foot house? You want to presume we will find a home on property that we can afford in a more expensive market, and create a new commute for me? And you want to start a horse rescue?"

I could feel myself shrink just a tad. *Well, yes, that pretty much covers everything.* Was he going to throw in my parents' disdain for the whole idea?

I'm going to digress here a moment. My parents cringed whenever plans displeased them. Life occurrences such as "I want to quit college" or "I want to move out of town" were met with silence and a confused glance, as if to convey, *what on earth would you do that for?* The thought of me kidnapping my children and moving 45 minutes way made for less than jolly conversation. I could see they were praying the whole idea would pass. It was no surprise. That was how things got handled when I was little, and those behaviors remain unchanged. If it was displeasing to mom or dad it could become a white elephant in the room. Ignored and not addressed, you ended up feeling a bit, well…lost.

I remember, when I was little, my sister told me she felt bad for me when it was time for me to go to kindergarten. I was only 4 years old. I wouldn't be 5 until the middle of November. She said she felt bad because I was so little she couldn't see the top of my head in the bus window. There she stood on the sidewalk waiting to see my head pop up, or perhaps the top of my head peeking above the windowsill. But no such luck. I couldn't wave goodbye because

I didn't dare kneel on the seat to see out that window. There I sat, bewildered, looking at the back of the dingy green bus seat in front of me.

Then, again in college, I had that lost feeling. I had no idea what to study or why I was going to college.

My mom said, "It doesn't matter what you study, just get a degree." I found this ambiguous advice less than helpful. How does one get a degree if they have no idea what they want to study? I wanted to save the whales and protest the building of nuclear power plants. Universities don't offer degrees in those kinds of interests.

My older sister had her goals and a plan laid out carefully. She'd already gone off to college, fallen in love, and was getting married. She'd eventually raise a family and get her master's degree. I envied her package. It was clear, concise, planned, and exactly what she wanted. But back then I didn't know what I wanted.

My younger brother followed in my father's footsteps. My father was a golf professional and he and my brother were best friends. When I was young, girls weren't allowed to play golf, or at least that's what I thought. Country clubs had restaurants in them, called The Men's Grill, where women weren't even allowed, and so I just accepted that women couldn't play the game either. If I liked it, or had a passion for it, I would never be given the chance for this discovery. It wasn't until I was older I learned that my father was afraid I would become a lesbian if I was allowed to play golf.

And so this was the experience I took from my childhood. I was loved, tucked in at night, told to value education, and be hetero-sexual. I was in the middle, floating through the haze, wondering where I fit in.

I would understand much later that what was difficult for me was managing both conversation and observation. Observation was an overwhelming task for me. While taking in all the movement around me, I wouldn't hear people talking to me, or the words being spoken around me. I would get lost in all the energy moving about. How people moved, where their hands were and what their eyebrows did, for me, was a language all by itself. The mundane chitchat at a party took backseat to watching the physical drama unfolding. To observe the pretty blonde brush against the arm of the man she is fantasying about all while placing a feigned "hello" kiss on his girlfriends' cheek, will scream at me over someone asking, "How are you Lynn, what's new in your world?"

I watched as friends and peers went through these social encounters like rituals. Body language has a rhythm and cadence all its own. I would observe and, for me, these events would play out in slow motion. Their voices would become like the adult voices I remember from Charles Shultz's A Boy Named Charlie Brown.

"Wha wha whawha wha…" I was immersed in the language of movement and energy. The words were superfluous. I didn't realize at the time that the ability to perceive, acknowledge, and understand the silent language of movement and energy was a gift. I learned later it is a prerequisite when working with horses.

Yet, for me personally, it remained a childlike state of curiosity when there is so much emotion and information to take in—all in a moment. And as a young adult, I still found myself feeling the same way. Overwhelmed, I didn't have a package. I felt like I was still 4 years old, sitting on the yellow bus.

"Ok, Let's make it happen."

A kiss on the cheek and he was gone, back into his garage. I was a bit taken aback. That's it? That's all it took? Wasn't he even going to remind me of all the pitfalls of such an adventure? Wasn't he going to remind me of all the reasons why we shouldn't make this happen?

It would be a big leap of faith. For a nanosecond, I thought, *am I ready for this leap?* Was my ever-present self -doubt going to set in and sabotage my effort? I was reminding myself and reviewing my thoughts over and over again. I realized I had already made the jump emotionally. It was too late for doing an about face. The emotional seeds of change had been planted, and the sprouts of a new adventure were pushing up through the soil of reality. I was already on my way, and then I got it. Dave had already realized it too. Life is one big bold adventure. Onward!

His buy-in was a moment for me to reflect on the beautiful treasured relationship I enjoy with this man. He is quiet, yet adventurous. He is trusting and concerned at the same time. He has the capability of addressing the fears and doubts of such an undertaking without diminishing the dream. I paused to thank God for sending me such a beloved human being.

Selling the house, dealing with realtors and messy children, will drive anyone mad. We haggled and countered, and with a "sold" sign hung out front, found ourselves landing in my brothers' lap on the coast. I grew up on the beaches in Santa Cruz County, and had watched the Santa Clara Valley become Silicon Valley. Coastal living appealed to all of us, and my brother was a gracious host.

What we found as we began to house hunt was very depressing. California real estate is expensive, and coastal real estate gets downright insane! I learned quickly to forget the dream house with all those wonderful amenities like granite countertops and gleaming hardwood floors. I had to forget a warm and cozy barn with huge turnouts. My dream of horses hanging their heads into the center aisle for social hour would have to be put on hold. I was determined just to find a house with a lot of dirt! I was ready to move into a shoebox, as long as there was property for horses. I gauged just how steep a hillside could be before a horse would tip over. I was creating bedrooms out of closet space. One house only had an outhouse for restroom facilities. Things were looking bleak.

It was a lovely sunny Saturday and we were driving on a picturesque road in beautiful Larkin Valley. The horse fencing lined both sides of the little two-lane road as it meandered along, clearly in no hurry. Every home had horses, cattle or goats dotting their green pastures. It was beautiful. It was perfect. It was also out of our price range.

I refused to panic. Just because I had sold our home, uprooted our children, imposed my family of four upon my brother, and created a new commute for my husband was no reason to panic, or so I told myself. We were three weeks into our shopping, and I was feeling, well, go ahead and say it: panicked!

Our Saturday drive led us to a beautiful ranch style home on 3 acres of poison oak. Decorated in vintage 1979 avocado green and harvest gold, we wandered through 2,700-square-feet of house. Three levels, two fireplaces, a big deck, and a view to die for were just what my soul had ordered. But the price tag was prohibitive. It was a mere $400,000 above what we could afford. We thanked the realtor for indulging us and drove back to my brothers.

Miracles come in many different fashions. Our little gift came to us through the telephone. The homeowner had called and wanted to know how we liked the house. *OK, that's odd, as homeowners don't do that.* Their representing realtor handles that stuff. My brother, David, who was our representing realtor explained how we loved it, how it was perfect for our two kids, for all the horses we were going to save, blah, blah, blah. I sat on the couch wondering why he was wasting his breath. Then there was silence.

"Really?" David said. He looked at us in surprise. My curiosity soared.

What? What? I was whining inside. *Tell me!*

"Four," he responded. Then his lip curved in disbelief. "Ok, I'll be right over to write it up."

He hung up the phone, "Congratulations, you just bought your house and got it for a mere $400,000 under their asking price!"

Elation is an inexplicable feeling…Jumping up and down screaming, "Oh Boy! Oh my God, we did it," may have been just the start. I began running around in circles. Packing, I needed to get packing. Wait! No packing. I was still packed! I realized I hadn't really unpacked. I was ready to go!

The weeks that followed roared by. Moving in and getting the kids set up for school. Moving Rose and her new baby girl over to the property, and making sure she had a nice secure area, kept us pretty busy. We were so excited to feel like we were in our home. Our whole family was here—the kids, the dogs and the horse. We had a horse! Before I could even exhale, my work to create Pregnant Mare Rescue had begun.

CHAPTER 7

Dazzle Me!

I had lists of the all the paperwork I needed to do: A Mission Statement, By–Laws, Articles of Incorporation, Standard Operating Procedures, Volunteer Agreements, Liability Release Forms. I needed that non–profit number!

Our new little 3-acre ranch had only one pasture. It was a makeshift area of T-stakes, wire, a little wood fencing, and a gate. I was putting together plans to erect nice board fencing and set up shelter before the winter season.

The Lone Star State of Texas found me and asked the question. Did we have room? Rescued from a Canadian Premarin farm was a mare with a foal at her side in need of a home. The promised home had backed out and this pair needed a place to go. This call tugged strongly at my heart, as I understand the horrors this mare has witnessed simply by coming off one of these farms. Let me explain.

Each year 75,000 mares throughout North Dakota and Canada are impregnated and confined to cramped stalls so their estrogen-rich urine can be collected for use in a drug called Premarin. It is a Hormone Replacement Therapy (HRT) for menopausal women. For six months, while their bodies are producing the most estrogen, these mares are unable to take more than a step or two in any direction, turn around, or even lie down. Lameness and muscle atrophy often develop. So that they can be put right back into production the next winter, the mares are re-impregnated when their first foal heat (availability to get pregnant) arrives. Within a few months, they are separated from their foals and put back on the "line." Fertile mares may go through this grueling cycle year after year.

At the tender age of 4 months old, the foals—all but a few who are kept for stud purposes or to replace worn out mares—are sold to slaughter. Mares are used in this practice until they drop dead on the line. Once the mares are so worn out that they become unable to conceive any longer, then they too are sent to slaughter. It is unfortunate that money is king because soy alternatives exist and are readily available. The alternative could eliminate this drug and the animal abuse in its entirety. This is the reality of "estrogen farming." Without hesitation we said "yes" and planned for their arrival. We were prepared with hay and a nice pasture waiting, but not much could have prepared me for meeting these horses.

Thick and round, she was marshmallow white with one big butterscotch patch on her flank and another on her face. Her deep brown eyes blinked at me, and her white and silver mane Rapunzeled its way down her thick neck. She was solid and sturdy like an old oak tree. Dazzle was a paint and Belgian cross mare.

She had been bred to a black Percheron stallion and her foal was the size of a small barn, standing upon hooves the size of dinner plates. She disembarked off the trailer and took in her surroundings. *Whoa,* I thought, *I hope she's sweet.* I meekly acknowledged my passing thought, *Cause if she's not, I may be dead.* Enormous, dark as night, and extremely hairy with a set of coal black eyes, I wondered if she wasn't part wooly mammoth. Her left ear must have been stepped on shortly after birth. Now permanently facing outward it gave her the appearance of always listening to the left. This foal arrived without a name but it became clear to me immediately she would be called Lil'Dozer, as in Little Bulldozer. She stood and waited for instruction.

We three began our trek up the long driveway to the ranch. I noticed the foal went to work being serious and cautious. She followed momma's lead. I had never experienced walking alongside draft horses. I noticed I wasn't really alongside so much as under when I looked up to see the underside of their jaws as we walked climbing the hill. Slow and steady these two girls were the pictures of quiet obedience.

I was completely silenced by their enormity. How strong could these horses possibly be? Their nostrils flared ever so slightly as they methodically placed one leg forward followed by the next. Feeling them inhale and exhale, I observed every nuance and noticed I was walking in rhythm with them. The sparsely graveled road crackled underneath their hooves. As we paused at the top of the hill, they again waited for my instruction.

"OK girls," I began, "Let me show you your new home." Surprisingly Dazzle threw her head up and down. A quick shake from side to side and she had very clearly conveyed her pleasure. I took just a moment to admire the flimsy little T-stake fence—it would be like holding elephants back with yo-yo string. I thought, better move the new fence up on the priority list of to-dos. These girls are a tad…hefty.

I opened the gate. As soon as halters were off, and there wasn't a moment's pause, they went bucking and thundering to the far end of the pasture. With an effortless extended trot, Dazzle made it from fence to fence in about eight strides. Now the real snorting began and the nostrils flared wide open. I stood at the fence watching their grace and taking in the beauty before me. These giant beings, so huge and bulky, could indeed be the image of poetry in motion.

Overtime we all would get to know Lil'Doz, and enjoy her baby brain antics. While her size made her a bit of an attraction, she still carried herself like the silly 3-month-old foal that she was. As she relaxed into her new digs, her curiosity and behavior kept us in stitches. I came to understand and experience for myself that draft horses, as I have read so often, are of a gentle nature beyond description.

It was a foggy afternoon and I had been struggling with the stress of paying the bills on time. It's a constant burden, but is bigger and more cumbersome at times. The garbage bill had not been paid and the quiet husband had to load the still full trash cans into the back of the wet truck bed and haul them back up the hill and to the side of the garage. Ugh, it was a disgusting smelly task. I was furious at myself for slipping up, not juggling the finances well, and causing David such an inconvenience. I began to feel sorry for myself because money can be so difficult and the frustrations so mounting. I found myself exploding into tears and heading to the pasture.

Rose and Lil'Doz began to make their way over to me but that was not to be allowed. Dazzle burst onto the scene chasing the two of them to the far corner of the fence line. She very deliberately and calmly walked up to me. She lowered her head and maneuvered around to my side. I fell into her mane and sobbed a trough's worth of pent up tears. She stood quietly and comforting while I shared all my frustrations and explained how badly I felt. She never flinched. She just stood and loved me. I began wiping my tears in her mane and thanking her. Her comfort, her love, her patience, and steadfastness were greater than her size. I looked into her eyes and saw such love.

"It's just a smelly garbage can Lynn. Dave is OK with it. It doesn't matter. You have given my baby and I safety and love. I look up to you every day. I am proud of you. You are my hero, Lynn. Please do not put my hero down. You belong to me. You are my friend."

I looked into those deep eyes once more. They twinkled and blinked. I was silenced and dumfounded. Did I make that up? Nope. Not possible. I paused and stared. Well, OK then. I wiped my nose and thought maybe I would listen to horses.

CHAPTER 8

How Did We As Humans Get So Derailed?

The energy and mood of my life shifted being in the company of horses so many times a day. These sneaky little creatures have a subtle influence on you and it's often not recognized for months. Then Kaboom! Ba'bing! The light bulb goes off. Grounding, being present, centered, setting your intention—all these statements when speaking about sharing space with horses makes sense. And once these statements begin making sense, the miracles begin to flow. The communication grows and the bond begins. It's stunning to experience. I was now finding myself observing noticeable problems with people and their horses everywhere I went. All those comments made big sense to me now and I had to bite my lip as I watched the quiet struggle. Tacking up (getting ready to ride), leading, riding, and unsaddling are all parts of riding I was suddenly observing with a grimace. The horses were so bullied and unhappy.

I decided to go back and do some research on horses and their role in societies with relationship to humans. If at one time people got on well with horses, where did it go wrong? I quickly located that over the course of history there are two noted relationships between man and horse that existed and provide confirmation for me that the human-horse connection, or better defined as a mutual respectful partnership, existed. If there are two that I am aware of, there surely must be many more hidden in the layers of history.

The first: Europe in the Middle Ages or medieval period lasted from the 5th to the 15th century. It began with the fall of the Western Roman Empire and merged into the Renaissance and the Age of Discovery. It has been observed and well documented that in these medieval times of knights and their mounts, the relationship of a Knight with his War Horse was held in the highest honor. A knight on a horse was a fearsome opponent. Medieval knights all used Destriers, and these horses played an extremely important role in their lives. These horses spent years training in partnership with their knight, as both of their lives would depend on this partnership. They were inseparable. Not enough can be stated about the nobility, presence, respect and reverence given to knights and their trusted steeds. Knighthood in the Middle Ages was closely linked with horsemanship as knights had to "protect the weak, defenseless and fight for the general welfare of all." They also had to act in courteous, chivalrous and honorable behavior. The word "chivalry" actually comes from the French word "chevalier" implying "skills to handle a horse."

No precise numbers exist, but it is estimated that at the order's peak there were between 15,000 and 20,000 Templars, of whom about one-tenth were actual knights. The Book of the Order of Chivalry, written in 1275 by Ramon Llull, describes the symbolism of every piece of the knight's equipment, saying clearly about the warhorse: "The horse is given to the knight to signify the nobility of courage so that he may be mounted higher than other men" (Lulle, ed. 1990, p. 58).

The use of the horse was essential to the use of the lance, for the power of its impact is determined by its speed and its strength; the rider's job consisting in maintaining the correct position, controlling the horse, and aiming at his opponent. This was very difficult and required extensive training from childhood and could only be practiced efficiently by those who had the time and money to afford such training. Warhorses likewise required special training. First, they needed to become acclimatized to the sounds and violence of combat. Secondly, for the couched lance technique, they had to accept running directly toward another rider (a rather unnatural thing for a horse), while also galloping on the right lead for the meeting. Indeed, the gallop is an asymmetrical gait, and by galloping on the right lead (the right front leg advancing and touching the ground in a forward direction to a greater extent than the left one, used by the animal to keep its balance in curves), it could compensate for an impact coming from its left. This special training may be an explanation for the name destrier, translated as "right-handed horse."

Because the momentum of the moving horse actually gave the blow its power, the horse also had to learn to push and to absorb the blow given to its rider. Warhorses were selected to be tall, fast, maneuverable, and strong enough to both give and receive blows. That is why the lance, until the very end of the practice of chivalry, remained the most knightly of weapons; only a knight with long practice on a costly trained horse could use it efficiently.

All of these technical explanations are important for understanding the relationship between these horses and the creation of the notion of chivalry, and as to why the warhorse was considered to be the knight's true double in representations (both pictorial and literary). Impressive, yes?

The second: Native Americans believed the bond between horse and rider to be sacred and that these two spirits became one. Native American Folklore tells a story about Sacred Medicine Hat horses: they are sacred, supposed to have special powers, and are very rare. The original medicine horse is almost entirely white, but has a colored patch covering the ears and the top of the head. This makes for a remarkable looking horse. Although a Medicine Hat horse may have other markings such as a spot over its chest, its shield, it is stated that the less markings they have the more powerful they were believed to be. The distinguishing head markings are what make up the Medicine Hat, or war bonnet, and those with one or more blue eyes are especially prized. Legend also states a Medicine Hat horse holds magical abilities to protect its rider from injury or death in battle, and to find wild game hiding in forests or canyons.

Tribes would steal the Medicine Hat horse of another tribe, believing that in doing so they would have the horse's good luck, stealing the fortune of the other tribe. A Medicine Hat horse was closely guarded by a tribe, and considered much more than a "good luck charm."

The relationship between the Native American man and his "pony" is for some Native American wives a contentious one at best. The pony often shared space in the tipi on stormy nights! In our minds we think of Native Americans and horses forever linked on the plains of the Wild West and life on the land all over the nation. But the truth of history reveals that the relationship of Native Americans and horses lasted over a short period of time. The days of Indian horsemen lasted a little over a century.

So when did the horses become primarily tools and servants to mankind? I think the bigger question is: when did the human ego get ahead of the importance of relationship and trust? There's the ever-present question of all time. It has been stated by some that horses are here on earth for us to use, and animals are here for us to eat. I find no truth in either statement but it begs the question, " Says who and what if you're wrong?" The queries began rolling in my head, one after another. How did a mass ignorance occur when it comes to handling, training, and riding these magnificent creatures? Where is the appreciation? Can't people see how miserable these animals are? Do they know what they are truly capable of?

With a bit more research, I found a chronological list of titled "Horse Eras" outlining how horses have served humans over the course of history. It would seem horses have ALWAYS been serving man, and perhaps the partnership based on trust and relationship is only now beginning to be recognized once again. That certainly would explain the lack of real skill that pervades the horse world. Lets take a look at how horses have served us throughout millennia.

- Era of Consumption (50,000 B.C.–present)
- Era of Utilization and Status (4000 B.C.–A.D. 1900)
- Era of Herding (3500 B.C.–present)
- Era of the Chariot (1700 B.C.–A.D. 400)
- Era of the Cavalry (700 B.C.–A.D. 1942)
- Era of Agriculture (A.D. 900–945)
- Era of the Carriage (A.D.1700–1920)
- Era of Leisure (1900–present)

To summarize, I discovered there is a plethora of information that is abundantly available with the click of a mouse, or touch on a tracking pad. Extremely simplified for obvious reasons, I can confidently state that horses have been with humans, and our development of civilization literally every step of the way. So, I ask why are we still eating and abusing them? The treatment is less than desired from my point of view and, according to this chronological history, we should now be in a period of *leisure*.

I tucked my thoughts and questions into my back pocket and refocused on our new rescues. I do believe answers often arrive in subtle ways and over time. Perhaps this huge question on the treatment of our beloveds need not be rushed and the answers would reveal themselves by me exhibiting patience.

While we were enjoying the amusement of living large with draft horses, Rose's little filly Roxy was busy growing up. She was now weaned and heading to a new home in Southern California. A teenage boy living on the edge of a desert town was anxiously awaiting his new partner in life. With all the background checks and home checks done, we tearfully bid farewell and good luck to Little Roxy. She was the very first horse adopted into a home by Pregnant Mare Rescue. We were so proud.

It was time for us to turn our attention to evaluate Rose. We knew she moved rather slowly and was a little different than other horses. We wanted to make sure she was OK. We took a trip to the Steinbeck Equine Hospital in Salinas for an evaluation. The X-rays and diagnosis summarized what was long suspected. She had suffered blunt force trauma to the skull. In other words it was highly plausible someone had hit her over the head with something very large—think baseball bat or a two-by-four. Her skull had a hairline fracture, and part of her vision may have possibly been damaged. They concluded that Rose probably has permanent brain damage.

The diagnosis would explain how she seemingly moves in slow motion as it is a bit of an anomaly. One moment she is inching along the fence rail heading toward the water trough, and her plodding along suggests she has trouble seeing. She'll step right in feeding buckets and any other object in her path. Yet, another moment later, she is standing alert, ears pricked, looking at a bicyclist way down yonder along the road. How can that be? It remains a mystery.

One late Friday afternoon, Scott, an awesome friend, came over to do some tractor work. We shuffled the pasture horses into a large quickly set up corral and closed them off. Oops! We forgot Rose! She was standing way up on the far hillside soaking up the sun.

"No worries," I said. "She'll stay put. Even if she heads this way it could take her all day to get to the opened gate".

So, off I went about my day. Scott revved up the old workhorse and began the task of moving manure and dirt around. I returned to the ranch after running my errands to find everything all tidy. Scott had moved the manure pile and all looked lovely. It was then I noticed a cute little fanny sticking out of my hay shed.

"What the heck?"

There was Rose. She had ever so delicately stepped into the shed, each hoof perfectly placed between the wood palate boards, her head stuffed in the hay. She had migrated across the pasture in what must have been record-breaking speed!

"Well, well, aren't we clever. Come on Rose, snack times up."

I grabbed an apple and she lifted her head. I could see her thinking…

"Ah, yes…Dessert?" Her nose works just fine and the aroma of fresh apple was enticement enough. She gently backed herself out as nicely as she had parked herself in and followed me out to the pasture. As I gently closed the gate behind her, I noticed the two other equines stood there in incredulous disbelief.

I simply had to chuckle to myself. This little quarter pony mare, diagnosed with a brain injury, never misses a meal. Rose has a very special place in our hearts as her sweet disposition defines her. She is kind, patient…and everything an orphaned, sick, little foal could wish for. The universe, Spirit, my God, always has perfect timing. Rose was about to get her first job.

CHAPTER 9

ISPMB

By the fall of 2008, Karen Sussman of North Dakota-based ISPMB, International Society for the Protection of Mustangs and Burros, inquired if I could possibly take four orphan mustang foals. Winter was on its way and times were already very tough out in the Midwest. They were experiencing an early winter season and mustang roundups were in full swing. The roundups are conducted by the BLM (remember the Bureau of Land Management). This is an extremely hot issue and a contentious one at best. Should mustangs and burros be removed from publicly held lands? By definition, a mustang is a free-roaming horse of the North American West that has descended with Iberian and Spanish bloodlines. Back in 1971 our United States Congress recognized mustangs as "living symbols of the historic and pioneer spirit that defines the West." It was also stated that these horses enrich the lives of the American people.

With that statement proclaimed, presumable protection in place, and horse lovers showering the government with praise, it becomes shocking to learn that our beloved mustangs are in grave danger. The very organization given the important task to protect and manage the wellbeing of these horses is eradicating them off our plains at record speed. The BLM, that government agency Dianne at the Wild Horse Sanctuary had mentioned, now questions the need for these animals to exist. Heated controversy surrounds this topic. The BLM wants our publicly owned lands to continue to be shared and used by private livestock holders and ranchers. The voice of the American people had voted to protect the horses. But politics are nasty and the roundups continue. The problem is escalating and with helicopters being used to run down and corral these terrified animals, I feel by the time the issue is solved…it may be too late. For me it remains a very sad circumstance. I think of the Buffalo.

My little Pregnant Mare Rescue had room available for Karen's orphans and so we began the task of raising money to haul the little ones down to Santa Cruz. We marked our calendar for November, but it would be February before the driver could get a rig into the North Dakota winter. To navigate the treacherous roads and horrendous weather, load four scared and untouchable babies, haul them safely in freezing conditions, and then deliver them to California is an enormous undertaking. Oh, did we mention that we'd like a discounted rate? So many things could possibly go wrong. It would boggle the mind if you allowed yourself too much thought. Sane people don't do this.

Each week I would receive a phone call with the latest news, "I'm sorry Lynn. Pass just closed, can't get in or out—could be three days, maybe longer."

"Ok, weather is supposed to break next week. Keep trying!" I tried my best to remain hopeful. The following week and another message is left on my phone. The static on the line and diesel engines rumbling in the background compete with a broken voice.

"Till bad, I'll kee…trying. Forec… for more …ow."

I could almost feel the icy cold and smell the grease. And so I waited. Karen's landline worked pretty well and although she had no better updates, I had learned that one of our orphans was being bottle fed in her living room.

The mother was found dead in a snowdrift, the foal lying next to the frozen carcass. Another 20 minutes and both would have been completely covered by snow. It would be late next spring before their bodies would have been discovered. But fate smiled upon this small filly as Karen had spotted its little head barely bobbing in the wind. Lifting 85 to 100 pounds of frozen horse in subzero temperatures is not for the faint of heart. A *heave* and a *ho*…and up on the seat…the foal landed. Karen quickly shut the door just in case she could make a break for it. That was highly unlikely as she was so cold and confused. Karen realized she had been out there in the elements alone too long. She was in distress.

Whisked into the warmth of the house, all her vital signs were checked. Yes, there was a little girl in there. She appeared half frozen, dazed and in pretty compromised shape. Karen began towel rubbing her little body.

"Come on little angel," she whispered. "Don't give up now."

Moments passed and up jerked a head. This was a good sign. Wrapped up tight in a warm blanket, the foal watched as Karen moved about the room. After a quick call to the vet, warm foal formula was on the way. Picking up baby's head and positioning herself to be able to bottle-feed her, Karen got comfortable on the floor. The first few slurps were tentative, followed by a mighty push to position herself square on the lap of her feeder. The warm meal was eagerly devoured!

Foals are full faculty births. This means that within minutes of being born they can see, hear, stand, walk, and eat. Mother nature has built in mechanisms for protection. Because they are prey animals, not predators, these capabilities make it possible for mom to foal (have her baby), drop her placenta, and then take baby and move on out. There is nothing quite as enticing as fresh placenta to a predator. In less than an hour, foals can and do use those long, lanky, uncoordinated limbs. It's an amazing thing to observe. It's incredible to witness if you're in the great outdoors, and just a tad worrisome if you're in your living room wondering when baby is going to spring to life! The foal slept with a warm tummy full of milk. Karen welcomed the vet—and began baby proofing her living room before all hell broke loose!

It was Christmas Eve and back in California we were all gathering at my sisters. It was tradition in our family to celebrate on the eve of Christmas when everyone was dressed and feeling cordial. We often included neighbors and lifelong friends to join in the festivities. The actual holiday was reserved for my immediate family, complete with warm cocoa and pajamas all day long.

My niece had just had her first child eight weeks earlier. The house was abuzz with baby talk, baby laughter, and all the excitement a newborn brings. It was the first great-grandchild for my parents.

"He's a cute little fellow," Grandpa smiled from the comfort of the couch. Grandma pulled out her checkbook and asked if she could write him a check.

"He's good, mom," my sister shot me a puzzled look.

"Well, he's awfully sweet." She asked one more time, "What is his name?"

Each question was the same and asked in the same way as if it was the very first time it was being asked. It was the first night of concerned glances amongst my siblings and I. We dined by a warm fire and opened our gifts. We repeated ourselves politely over the course of the evening.

Christmas morning, my children, the quiet husband and I sat looking into one another's eyes. *What was happening to mom?*

CHAPTER 10

The Raccoons, Deer And My Awakening

Forward into February and we were chilly! Day after day, nature brought very cold, grey skies and lots of drizzle. We were still waiting on the orphans to arrive. Dave and I had enjoyed a roaring fire, a little television, and I was ready for sleep. I tucked in looking forward to my slumber, pulling a fluffy comforter up to my neck. *Ah, bedtime.*

Crash! Sounded like it was coming from the garage. Crash again! It sounded like a spinning piece of metal on concrete. *Hmmm.* I begrudgingly sat up and put on my robe. The quiet husband was, well, quietly sleeping. I opened the garage door and flicked on the light wondering what on earth could be making such a racket. To my surprise, and most certainly to theirs, was a family of raccoons! One sat inside the garbage can that we use for the dog food, his mask barely showing above the rim. I suspect what must have been chubby momma sat behind the opened garbage can with her paws upon the open rim. Two more little thieves sat on the ground, paws in the air, taking the doggie kibble as it was handed to them! Glancing over their shoulders at the intruder, they all locked their masked faces on me with that deer in the headlights look.

"Mayday, mayday! Bail!"

The momma chub went to work and reached in to pull her cub out by the scruff of his neck. Dropping him to the floor, he rolled a little on his side before regaining his upright position. I saw he wouldn't let go of his fistful of snacks. They waddled over to the doggie door and began pushing each other's full-figured fannies through the narrow exit as if to say "move it, mission aborted!" *Well, don't rush,* I thought. Their little fists never relinquished the kibble and they never took their eyes off of me. Exit stage left! One by one they disappeared out the door and into the night. I glanced over at the garbage can lid, strewn all the way across the garage.

What a mess! I picked up the remains of their feast and began to close up shop. *Dang, little critters.* I reminded myself to close the doggie door permanently.

Ah, back into bed. This time, I am ready to doze.

Clip clop, clip clop. I lay there with one eye open. Are you kidding me? Now what? Throwing back the covers, annoyed and freezing, I began swearing under my breath. I once again threw on the robe to go see what was happening now. We have boards right outside our bedroom window. They resemble an old Western walkway, the kind ol' cowboys used to frequent while they chewed their tobacco and spat into the dirt. Our boards make up the quickest route down to the lower pasture. I was imagining Rose meandering down in the drizzle to who knows where, and God only knows what for at this hour of the night!

Surprise again, it wasn't Rose but a mama doe and her two fawns. Little spotted butts glowing shiny and wet. I never knew deer had such big noses. *Geez,* I thought, *they must smell stuff from miles away.*

"Is this animal party night and I wasn't invited or what?"

They froze and I could see them wondering what move to make next. I froze too and let them decide, thinking all along about my geraniums! Just follow the path and you'll be safe and sound. Off they went doing that funny trot thing that deer can do. Momma and her fawns disappeared into the night, with my geraniums safe. I shook my head as I went inside thinking about how there's certainly never a dull moment when you share your life with animals... all kinds of them.

In the quiet stillness of the night, I pondered my thoughts as they drifted in and out of my sleepy haze. I believe I do my best thinking in the dark, lying in the unmoving silence of night. I reflect that animals just exist. They live in the moment and continue to remain honest, authentic, and in the present. This is extremely difficult for humans to do. I thought about the gang of partygoers in my garage looking for a meal. I thought about the way, year after year and decade after decade, these animals continue to achieve what humans should be considering: the task of living in the present. I observe that we as a human race have gotten so far from nature and from authenticity. I realized that is the draw for me. I began to see that, for me, this ranch, these animals, and these horses make it possibile to simplify my thoughts and to live in the moment. To be with horses will require returning to that childlike state of curiosity and to, once again, capture the ability to be present—because being present facilitates truth and trust.

It felt as though the floodgates had been opened. The clarity was blinding. For a instant I flashed back to all of the uncomfortable moments I had experienced. All of my self-doubt, self-degradation, and scolding could now be put away it seemed. There was purpose behind my struggle. Body language and nuance does have its place. There is a bigger, greater understanding for me about how this experience of life unfolds. I am indeed a spiritual being on a physical journey, and not the other way around. It felt like my world order had just shifted. I became important. How wonderful is that?

It was such a wonderful thought that I woke smiling and beaming with energy for the day ahead. A confusing grey cloud had dissipated and clarity was my new companion. *Full steam ahead, Lynn. You've got this!*

The Gila Herd, the Catnip Herd, and the White Sands Herd are just a few of the names of the beautiful, majestic, endangered wild mustang herds whose foals have made their way to our rescue here in California. The orphans from North Dakota, borne from these herds, finally made their debut in the middle of February. The bottle-fed baby had been named Angel. Karen had a special fondness for this little filly and I could see why. She was lovely and very spirited—a true wild mustang born on the North Dakota plains.

Angel, one of the four orphans, was a national treasure indeed. I would stand at the fence and observe. She romped and reared and held her head high in the air. This proud filly was unique in every way. She stood with enormous presence.

Her left ear was missing the tip—must have been frostbite. I was reminded how close she had come to not surviving. The three other foals were sweet and shy. A little filly, Janny, was the color of dirty snow. A pair of colts, both beautiful chestnuts with big white blazes running down their foreheads, made numbers three and four. They were fuzzy-coated bodies hiding fat bellies full of worms.

The first order was to get rid of the worms. So, as they began shedding their wildebeest appearance, they also began slimming down and shining. By late spring we had four beautiful foals, healthy and thriving.

An "umbilical hernia" is a kind of small birth imperfection that needs be repaired. The opening of the abdomen where baby was once connected to the placenta doesn't fully close. There is a small procedure that closes the opening. We discovered as we began touching our foals that one of our little chestnut boys had just that issue. A little bump under the fur on the underside of his tummy was a sure indicator. He would need surgery.

When you are only 12 weeks old these small procedures are a huge deal. I worried about him adjusting. I fretted about the little guy self destructing from stress. Foals rely on their moms for so much more than just milk. He came through the procedure just fine, and woke up in a cozy foaling stall with loving company. Can you guess whom?

Rose went to work settling and reassuring this little guy. Within minutes of his frantic awakening from the anesthesia, Rose had him quieted and content. This proved to be an incredible gift. His recovery time would be decreased, as there would be no drawbacks, no ripped stitches, and no problems. Rose became worth her weight (and there was plenty of that!) in gold. Eventually, one by one, all four foals would be adopted into their new homes.

A woman who held a keen interest in the origins and history of the mustang herds adopted Angel. The following was written from Angel's new mom, Shannon:

I've done some research in the Apache language, because I wanted an authentic Apache name for Angel. Her herd existed in traditional Apache territory and was the herd that the Mescalero tribe drew their horses from (also known as the wildest and tallest of all wild horse herds by the way). I am going to call her NITIKO... a female Apache name meaning "angel made of gemstone." In other words, an Angel of the heart who is beautifully formed. It does sound very close to the name she is used to here at the ranch (Nariko) and also honors Karen's first choice (Angel).

Shannon and Karen have been connected and I am happy to know they both share an interest in keeping "Nitiko" happy and healthy. Karen and the ISPMB continue their work keeping mustangs from the slaughter pipeline while educating the nation on the plight of our beloved national treasure, The Wild Mustang.

CHAPTER II

Kidnapped

I n 2009, the third summer of horse rescue, I found myself hijacked by two of the most important mentors in my life. The two women responsible for my kidnapping were a mighty powerful duo of guts, brains, ambition, and drive. Marlene is a retired policewoman, firefighter, and horse-person extraordinaire who runs her own rescue out of King City. Shirley, all by herself, has coordinated the rescue of thousands (yes, I said thousands) of horses. She is also the founder of NERN, The National Equine Resource Network. Truth be told I didn't know these women very well, only their sterling reputation in horse rescue that preceded their arrival. I was surprised as they stood on my doorstep paying an unexpected visit. They reassured the quiet husband that they would keep me safe, and that we were headed to Fallon to pick up seven horses and drop them at various locations around the state.

OK. I raised my eyebrows. And then they mentioned that we'd be back sometime tomorrow.

"Tomorrow?" I wondered if the astonishment was showing on my face.

It was 8:30 p.m. and Fallon, Nevada, was seven or eight hours away. "Tomorrow" translated to my understanding that we'd be driving basically the entire time.

Deep breath. OK then.

Loaded up and on the highway, I noticed the quiet landscape stretch out before me. Marlene always hauls at night. It's cooler for the horses, and she has the road to herself. I noticed she was correct. We were dead ass alone on the open highway. I looked around at the size of her enormous four-door dually, oversized luxury truck and took comfort thinking it was extremely unlikely that we'd encounter any mechanical problems. Though, just in case, I did two knocks on the fake wood on the console.

The moon was up and we blasted across the state of California heading east. Up over the Sierras and dropping into the Nevada basin put our arrival at just about 3 a.m. We had exhausted every conversation about horses imaginable and rolled into our motel room ready for sleep. We managed a whopping three hours.

Up at 7 a.m. and ready to roll, we headed to the Fallon Auction House, more affectionately known as "the feedlot." In the early days of horse rescue, rescue organizations used to be able to go to the lot the day after the auction to pick up their saves. Rumor has it that now the folks who run these auctions are so tired of the hysteria, and angry rescuers, that they don't allow rescues to pick up their saves until after the kill buyers have departed. (Gosh, can you imagine people being angry as they watch horses being terrorized and treated like meat products?) So, to avoid any inconvenience in their workday, the new rules apply. Kill buyers load up their horses and leave for the borders Tuesday. The saves we have purchased get picked up on Wednesday.

The horses that are sold to these so-called kill buyers have a price that is calculated by the pound. Mothers are torn away from their babies and families are separated. Geldings, stallions, mares, and yearlings all get thrown into the same mix. Sometimes their journey—without food or even a water stop—can easily last 18 hours. Stallions don't fare well with other stallions. Amidst the fear and chaos, many arrive dead or quite literally in pieces. I think that would be a blessing. I'd rather arrive dead than be subject to the tortures that would follow.

It's now Wednesday at 8 a.m. We are prompt and ready, and... we are kept waiting. I get bored easily and began to fidget.

I meander around and notice a dilapidated building adjacent to the lot. I stroll across the parking lot taking mental notes as I go. The door has a padlock and a "Keep Out" sign hangs on the door-knob. The windows are barred. Hmm, I think to myself. *What went on inside?* Casually, I step around back. There is ramp and a corridor. Decaying wood rails mark the trail. I walk the path. Bingo, what looks like the animal entrance is unlocked!

With a little nudge to the door, I slip inside. I stand in silence. I am in a dingy, poorly lit concrete building. Dried blood covers portions of the walls and most of the floor. I look down and see a drain. There is a big chain, rusted red, lying in the center. There was an enormous hook, about 18-inches long, strewn over in a corner. Glancing up I see metal rails. I imagine the hook connected to the chain, and the chain hanging from the rail. I think this is how a carcass must have been moved around. I can feel the dead lifeless body being rolled along the rails. I realize I am standing in the kill area of an equine slaughterhouse.

I feel the walls begin to whirl around me, becoming nearly a blur. My head felt hot and my stomach was lurching. It was then I got mad. Damn it! *I am not going to faint. For every last horse that lost its life in this God damned hellhole, I am not going down!* I was furi-ous. I closed my eyes and made it stop. STOP! I silently screamed at myself.

I opened my eyes. The dirty, bloodied walls stood unconcerned with my grief. I steadied myself and walked to the next room. There was a closet neatly lined with blood-soaked canvas jackets. It looks like they once might have been the color beige. Each had its own hanger, all facing the same direction. Some even had names. I read that Joe and Martin and Carlos had all worked in this place.

I wondered what they felt, and if they felt at all? Did they care about the horrors, the sadness, or the pain inflicted on these animals all day long, day in and day out?

Were they immune? How could one become immune? Perhaps they were dead inside? I pondered to myself. *What does it take to be able to work in this place?* So many unanswered questions lingered in the air, like the stench filling my nostrils.

I had seen enough. I left the same way I got in. I glanced at the racks lined with trays that I suspect once held the packaged meat products. I slipped out the door, and headed up the path back into the light of the day. I had just walked out of a room of death and agony—a room of torture and pain. I had just walked right out of hell.

I had researched enough to know that in November of 2007 the last horse slaughterhouse in the United States had been shut down. The butchering of our beloved American horses was finally ended. The U.S. slaughterhouses had been foreign owned, employed a mostly transient illegal workforce, and slaughtered upwards of 80,000 equines annually. It is fact that people in Asia eat horsemeat, and that is the market. It was no matter that American horsemeat is tainted with substances deemed toxic for human consumption. Every antibiotic, every vaccine, and all the routinely administered painkillers for our equines all state clearly on each and every label, "This product is not for animals intended for human consumption." It is no secret, yet this does not seem to deter the appetite for profit.

It is a misconception that horses go to the glue factory or get turned into dog food. I mean it's possible that some do. But the harsh truth is they are butchered alive and then packaged and shipped overseas. The horror stories vary as to how the butchering occurs. Better sit down. Parents, you might want to fast forward.

Each culture has its own beliefs and methods for butchering an equine. Head south to Mexico and a knife is used to sever the spinal cord. They torture and beat each horse prior to death, believing it makes for more tender meat. Head north and Canadian slaughter-houses use a captive bolt gun to stun right between the eyes. This gun was designed to stun cows, however, it can take many attempts to make this happen. Once stunned, they are hung from their back legs, then the front limbs are severed off and they are left to bleed out. Should they linger, being skinned alive in not uncommon. If they are not stunned then it's just too bad, as the process will continue like clockwork. I have been told that in bovine processing houses, the cow's limbs are often simply cut off if the animal, while being hung upside down, is flailing and their limbs are in the way of the workers. Some of the latest news shared is the heinous new trend in Japan. Live foals are transported by air directly to Japan and butchered as needed. They serve sashimi—raw baby horsemeat as a delicacy. Is anybody else sick to their stomach?

"You're not supposed to be over here!" I heard the voice loud and oh so clear.

"I'm sorry, I got lost," I said innocently.

"Well, you need to stay on that side of the parking lot. Your horses are ready for pick up."

"Thank you," was all I needed to say. I was blonde. I could be… blonde.

Marlene and Shirley were busy loading the horses onto the trailer. Six loaded, one to go. The last girl was a cute little chestnut mare. A little banged up, but she definitely had potential. Nice head and pretty butt, although she was frazzled as they all are when coming off of these death lots.

"Where you been?"

I wanted to answer "to hell and back" but I just shrugged. "Looking around."

The last mare loaded and we secured the door. *Bang! Oh no, that isn't good. Bang, Bang!* Our last little traveler was double barreling into the trailer wall.

Marlene yelled, "Get her outta there!"

Shirley and I scrambled to open the door. A second later the mare was being led back into the corral. There she stood on the other side of the fence line.

"Sorry, but I can't have her kicking the trailer," Marlene mumbled apologetically. A myriad of things could go wrong in an instant with one obstreperous horse. Broken legs, damaged equines, or a bloody mess in the middle of the open road is not an option. It is always safety first with horses. Hauling is inherently one of the most dangerous tasks to do with horses.

I thought, *ok…no big deal.* Then it hit me. Yes, it was a big deal! It was a huge deal! She didn't know! She didn't understand! She had made a mistake that just sealed her fate. She would not be going to a rescue. She would be kept until next week, and then shipped out. I stood there looking in her eyes. My heart was so heavy. *Oh my God, she would be sent to the slaughterhouse.* I was looking directly into the eyes of this live being and understood the horror she would be soon facing. The horror of slaughter now had a face.

I was at a loss for words. What is wrong with the world? I must have been close to comatose. Maybe I was crying. I wasn't sure. I felt arms wrapping around me, and a quiet, gentling voice nudging me, "Come, we must go."

The emptiness I felt was difficult. The lessons learned were brutal. One cannot save them all. All the brutality, all the hatred, and all the casual ways people justify the cruelty cannot be explained. There is little we can do but to put one foot in front of the other, and put one day behind us—always looking on to the next. I vowed to ignore how large a task this was and to continue one horse at a time. Every life saved does matter. I have looked into the eyes of that one horse.

It was in these moments as we headed out of Fallon that I learned what I was made of and just how strongly I felt about making a difference. I learned how strong I was…period. The little child on the back of the bus began to float away. I had a plan, I knew what I wanted, and it was very clear. Our American horses, our silent brave devoted partners throughout this lifetime, needed us. They needed every single one of us.

By the spring of our fourth year in rescue, Dazzle and Lil'Doz had been adopted into a loving home. I was happy to see them both go to the same wonderful person, although I have to say it was bittersweet. I wanted to keep Dazzle. I wanted to enjoy the gifts she shared, her love, and her quiet wisdom. But when you're working on 3 acres, collecting horses in not an option. Dazzle continues to visit me in a spiritual and magical way. Under the light of the full moon, I walk the grounds and reflect on all her amazing qualities. Her capacity to forgive and to serve is astonishing in today's world. I began to realize that horses are so much more than people understand. Dazzle taught me that they have so many gifts to share.

CHAPTER 12

A Thoroughbred's Fame and Fortune... Or Not

E ach morning, when the sun begins to show itself, I usually peek out the sliding door to see if anyone is in the lower pasture. Usually there is a body or two soaking up the first rays of warmth. They stand quietly, heads lowered in comfort. If they are young, I see them sacked out like baked potatoes lying in the warm earth.

Dave has long ago left for work. My children, Robert and Jillian, are sleeping and I am left to my own devices. Muddling around in the early morning sun is one of my most favorite things to do. I am usually a fashion statement at this hour in my most tired, red, faded bathrobe cinched tightly at the waist, dripping of hay particles. My boots meet the hemline and with a ponytail bobbing behind me, I am ready for the morning.

There they stand, "Well, good morning!"

The nickers begin as they greet me...letting me know they are indeed ready for breakfast. The first stop is to feed the Thoroughbreds. Las Vegas Dancer and Ballet Lesson are stunning, extra-large Thoroughbred racehorses. They hold prestigious lineage, each having earned respectable winnings on the track, and yet both found themselves discarded. Ballet was boarded at a barn experiencing a hostile takeover. Pregnant and abandoned, she came to me under threat of being sent to the auction house. Las Vegas Dancer was relinquished. Her owner didn't provide much information as to why, just asked if we could take her pregnant mare. She said she was sweet and bred to a lovely Thoroughbred stallion. She was delivered, along with her papers, like a UPS package on a Monday.

The third Thoroughbred was actually a gelding. The call came in from the San Diego area. The familiar story was shared. A woman boarding her horse at a racing stable had fallen on hard times. Her bill for training and board had reached a whopping $8,000! This big boy would now be on his way to a Mexican racetrack.

A good Samaritan explained, "His ransom is $1,000. Can you help?"

Well, this horse was a he, not a she, and was certainly not in foal. But it was no matter, as a Mexican racetrack isn't any life for a horse. The next morning, Jillian and I hooked up a borrowed trailer and with my husband's truck—and my own money in hand—headed out for the long drive to San Diego.

These trips are always small expeditions into the unknown. My daughter's lighthearted sense of humor, and her delight of a road trip, made our travelled miles fly by…even through the Los Angeles 405. We arrived at a most welcoming home. The woman greeted us with a warm smile and great appreciation for our mission. She had fronted the ransom money and, anxious to get him out of the barn, had hauled him to her ranch.

We rounded the stucco garage heading to the back area to find neatly trimmed grass bordering a row of paddocks. Beyond the paddocks was a fenced pasture backed by low hills in the distance. It was a lovely sunset. The evening air was warm like Southern California warm can be and the expansive views were welcoming. Two enormous horses grazed contentedly as we approached.

"This is Alamony." She smiled as the beautiful dark bay lifted his head acknowledging his name. A blaze of white slid all the way down his face. From his forehead, down past his bridge, the creamy color then made a right turn and slipped into his nostril. It looked like fresh cream running off the side of his face. I was quietly chuckling at the site of this most unusual blaze. We then learned that Alamony had an interesting story to share.

Born in San Diego, he was one of the 16 grandsons of Seattle Slew. Seattle Slew was an American Thoroughbred racehorse that won the Triple Crown in 1977—the 10th of just 11 horses to accomplish the feat. He remains the only horse to win the Triple Crown while undefeated. He was a superstar. His son, Slewvescent, had a prestigious record of his own, taking first place 14 times and earning more than $194,000 in his racing career. These findings created a mass interest in the newly rescued gelding. Prestigious barns sent in their resumes, bidding for the fancy grandson of a superstar. Phone calls poured in from across the nation.

We had committed sight unseen, promising a safe, loving home for life. While we knew nothing about him, we only knew he needed help. Fate had dealt him a tough blow, and we felt he deserved a second chance. We relished being the chosen ones and were so pleased to see his wellbeing put above fancy barns and deep pockets. We were giddy with joy knowing that this amazing equine would have the chance for a wonderful loving life.

It's a precarious fine line between being a fancy star and a rescued life. Same breed of horse, same super fantastic lineage, same breeding—and one horse ends up a star worth millions while the other, the grandson, is a $1,000 save from a life of hell. Luck may be the only differentiating factor.

Our trip home proved uneventful save for one wrong turn early on. The three of us ended up at the bottom of a ravine on a dusty road. We found a place on the side of the dirt road with an ever so sparse shoulder for me to begin my three-point turn. I only had to complete this turn 16 times to get completely turned around and headed back up the hill! Alamony was a patient passenger and soon enough we were back on our way home.

On this particular morning, breakfast found all three Thoroughbreds in good shape and ready for their day. I see great transformation in the horses that come to spend time here. Nothing is asked of them except to release the hurt and to heal. They release a lot of their anger and, unlike humans, have this enormous capacity for forgiveness. I don't know if it is because they live in the moment, or perhaps they are more evolved than we are as a species. But their healing is extraordinary. Once they understand that their lives are forever different and forever better, they heal. The trust that begins to show is a sure sign of the healing that's taking place. I can feel them exhale as if to convey, "Finally, someone who gets it."

The scared, mean, unhappy, and very pregnant mare has transformed herself into a loving, peaceful mother. This dangerous mare who lashed out at passersby became a mother who allows me access to her foal, and trusts me with her wellbeing and the wellbeing of her newborn. In more than 12 years—and more than 200 horses—I have never been charged at, injured, or threatened in the foaling stall. It is an unspoken bond between the mare and I. My promise is that I only assist and I do not interfere.

When Las Vegas Dancer, the oh-so-crabby Thoroughbred mare I mentioned, gave birth to "Leaving Las Vegas," or Leah, I had been keeping the night oil burning. In her discomfort, she seemed to appreciate the company as the hours passed. I spoke softly to her and she would lower her head and sigh. I took a quick bathroom break at 5:10 a.m., and four minutes later upon my return I discovered a brand new foal.

"You were just waiting for me to leave now weren't you?" Her soft nicker translated to "yes."

I remember that March morning was very cold and damp. I took a towel and began rubbing gently. Mom put her nose right next to little Leah as if to reassure her that all was well. Up she stood! This little girl has racing bloodlines and the legs to prove it. *Wow, the longest legs I've ever seen on a foal.* Newborns arrive rather stunned, looking mostly dazed and confused. What just happened? Well, you were born! I sat quietly in the shavings taking in this tiny miracle. She wobbled and leaned, took a step, and collapsed. Mom nickered and stepped in close. Up she went again. Determination is all she could muster, as I'm sure there was very little coordination going on. Her little tail was flicking back and forth, so short it barely touched her little rump cheeks. She began looking for milk. Step and lean, sniff and suckle. She started at mom's shoulder and worked her way down her flank. In frustration she flicked her tail harder and then came a stomp.

"Oh my!" She surprised herself. She looked down at herself as if to think, "Hmmm, these things must belong to me, how convenient!"

The realization that the legs were hers was but a moment's distraction. Back to the milk hunt she went. She unintentionally slipped her nose under mom's belly. I leaned forward to peek underneath and caught the most hilarious sight. There she stood in complete disbelief. A milk shower was pouring from mom's teats and baby now had eyelashes dripping of the liquid warmth. In an instant, her mouth began suckling loudly and slurping her first meal. With baby up and nursing, I decided I could go find my nice warm bed. I grabbed the foal blanket and ever so gently draped it over Leah's back. Mom leaned over and took it right off with her teeth and dropped in on the ground.

"OK," I smiled. "You're the mom."

Slipping quietly under the bedcovers, I tried not to disturb the quiet husband. The silence in the country at night is as big as the night sky itself. It wraps around you and tucks you in like a sleepy child. My cocoon is warm and safe. I lay in the darkness and pondered. *A brand new life—a perfect little girl has arrived.* I thought of how fortunate she and her mother are to be here with us. They came close to a horrific ending. All rescues have understood the feeling of abandonment. They all understand loss. A lucky few will understand healing love and peace.

As I tried to fall asleep I imagined a place where equines were in scarce supply. A place where it was unheard of that a horse—a gorgeous powerful generous equine—would ever end up discarded, unwanted at a rescue or, God forbid, on the slaughterhouse floor. They were valued and cared for, and there was a waiting list to acquire one. The list couldn't be bought or sold, bribed or cheated upon. The coveted list remained pure. Names that landed on the list had passed a rigorous inspection. Love, care, loyalty, trust, acknowledgement of equine greatness, and pride of ownership all were conditions of ownership. Horses were more valued than gold and highly respected. I think it was the list from Rainbow Bridge. I think I got a peek of how it's supposed to be. Off to sleep I drifted.

Here at Pregnant Mare Rescue these horses have found a safe place. These three Thoroughbreds have shown me a greatness of heart, an amazing capacity for forgiveness, and have provided a lesson in how to trust. The horses spent all spring and summer season here and enjoyed being treated like royalty. All three are now in wonderful homes, and the love and care continue.

CHAPTER 13

Work Hard! Work Long Hours For No Money, Smell Bad And Laugh, You Are Now A Volunteer!

The volunteer force is such an extremely important facet of the work we do here at the rescue. Educating the people and saving equine lives is an enormous undertaking. My blessings appear as I have the good fortune of making fabulous life-long friendships.

Volunteers are the backbone of the labor force at the rescue. This project of saving lives could not function without the help of this mighty group of people. Horse chores such as mucking and feeding, checking waters, and grooming are the coveted tasks. Touching and hanging with the horses for many is the reward. But I have an army of committed folks handling the books, the budget, the fundraising, the fence fixing, the training, and the grant writing. The amount of daily work is endless. Our social network is extremely valuable when we need to raise emergency funds, and keeping up with all the current social outlets takes time. I have one volunteer that focuses on checking in on each horse we have saved.

Every year, each horse needs to be checked in with and we like to make sure all is well. It's an enormous amount of work and my rescue is a small one. Protecting those without a voice is a big task.

Katy and Scott are dear friends who came into our lives because of the horses. Katy adopted my very first orphan foal pulled off the lot from Fallon. These friends have the biggest, most generous hearts one can imagine.

In the very early days of rescue, we managed on a shoestring budget and finagled anything we needed by being extremely creative. Katy was well aware that winter was going to bring rain, and rain was definitely going to bring mud. Now, it is not secret that at times I can be very blonde. "Ditz" is a title for me that might come to mind. Katy had mentioned a couple of times that the rain was coming and that I had better prepare. I must have looked like a confused squirrel wondering where I had hit my nuts for the winter. I kept thinking, *I know I have to do something, just don't know what.*

Katy took charge. She and Scott picked up the quiet husband and I, and off to the pumpkin patch we headed. Katy had worked her magic and with permission we took all the left over straw bales that the pumpkin patch owner no longer needed. We drug, wrestled, and rolled square bales of straw end-over-end and then onto a borrowed flatbed. Midway through our task, a light rain began to fall. What began as tiring work became a hysterical effort to get this stuff home before it was all soaked and twice as heavy! Piled in the truck and heading home, we smelled like wet, muddy rats and looked like backcountry mountain folk with straw strands sticking out of our hair.

We managed to get back to the ranch and Katy and I proceeded to spread the straw all over the ground. Like little girls we were throwing it high above our heads and watching it float down. It looked like snow. Two acres covered in straw is beautiful. The rain then began to really pour. Laughing was the only thing left for us to do. We had done it…Erosion Control 101! Katy and Scott have years more experience in horse keeping, and their experience continues to remind me that I have much to learn. I thank God for dear friends!

We did experience a volunteer nightmare once and, unfortunately, it involved my daughter. Jillian is very protective of her boy, an older Arabian named Whiskey. She dotes and fusses on him with all the care a mother gives her newborn child. Part of Whiskey's appeal is his undeniable charm. His forelock (bangs) hangs down well below his eyes, almost to the middle of his head. He is blessed with a gorgeous mane and a sporty little physique. Did I mention he is 29 years old? Charming as hell. He nuzzles up and rests his head on your shoulder, and wiggles his nose right into your heart. He will make you feel as if you may be his most important person in his world.

I came home one afternoon to hear shrieks from the back area. I dropped everything to go see what the accident was. *Oh God, I thought, please don't let anyone be hurt.* I rounded the corner and stopped dead in my tracks.

Oh dear, this is not good. We have, I should say had, a new volunteer. He didn't follow directions very well and took a few action items upon himself. And so there we have it. Whiskey stood at the hitching post. His Fabio forelock had been chopped. He had little boy bangs. I think it's called a bowl cut. His beautiful long sexy surfer hair was gone. He looked like the Dutch boy on the paint cans.

"Oh dear," I mumbled aloud. "I'm so sorry. Um…it will grow back."

My pitiful comment was no help.

"I'll kill him." Jillian was fuming. "Better yet I'll shave his head. Where does he get the idea thinking this would ever be OK?"

I was silent. I didn't have any answers. I was actually wondering the same thing. I added, "Try not to laugh at him. You'll hurt his feelings."

Jillian shot me that glare only teenagers possess. Unhappy and frustrated, she put Whiskey in his paddock. The next four weeks, every time we went out back to the horses, he stood with his butt facing us. Don't tell me they don't understand. He was furious too.

I also will never forget the afternoon I came home to find a large chestnut gelding with half of his cheek skin hanging off his skull. He had gotten into a spat with the gate hinge and lost. I immediately called the vet and took to keeping "Red" as comfortable as possible until help arrived. In the midst of this emergency a fairly new volunteer arrived to muck his pasture. This woman was horrified at the sight of this poor bloody horse doing his best to patiently stand with me.

The vet inquired, " How bad, Lynn?"

I replied, "Eight on a 1 to 10. It is not pulsing blood, but we are pretty steadily bleeding. Better rush."

"I'm on my way."

Relief was 15 minutes out. I began to breathe.

I asked our newer volunteer not to muck, as it would kick up dust and debris. In that instant she began explaining to me how she doesn't deal well with blood, or emergencies. I told her it would be fine for her to go up above to the horses and work there. She stood frozen in her tracks. She began to speak faster and louder. I was beginning to feel nauseated. I needed her to leave. More words came flooding out of her mouth. Her words were flowing faster than the blood I was trying to help coagulate. The vet and her assistant couldn't get here soon enough.

Poor Red had punctured a hole in the bone of his jaw. A portion of the gate hinge had shattered a piece of the jawbone, and the vet was concerned about drainage and infection. I have two fabulous veterinarians. I am eternally grateful for their timely, professional and compassionate help. Dr. Terry eventually discovered that his nostril cavity miraculously was acting as a drain. The risk of infection setting in because of stitches would not be a problem, and no drain would be necessary. Relaxing with a bit of good news, I began to hear this low buzzing sound in the background. I stood concentrating on what the vet was telling me. I focused harder, staring at the vet's lips as instructions were being given to me. Still, a voice continued droning on like an old buzzing refrigerator. With Red now sedated and out of pain, I took in my surroundings. She was still standing there…and she was still talking. *Oh my God*, I thought, *quit babbling woman, shut up!* It was difficult but I refocused, once again, my efforts on the vet and received my instructions. I made sure my instructions for Red were clear and promptly made a beeline to the house. I needed relief! Now I could hear her talking to the vet as I disappeared. I felt bad leaving the vet alone to manage the onslaught of verbiage coming at her. But selfishly I made peace knowing the vet would be leaving soon. I took a deep breath and let out a sigh as I wondered if I was the only person who can physically become sick with too much language. She will forever be known as I teasingly nicknamed her "The Babbling Mucker." I chuckled to myself thinking the blood was too much as this was her last visit to the rescue. Red happily made a full recovery. I did, too.

A young student from the University of California at Santa Cruz had made a telephone call into the rescue. She shared she was a biology major; she was interested in obtaining large animal experience. What I had yet to observe was the talent and tenacity this young woman was about to display. She rode her bike to the bus stop, took a bus all the way to the south end of the county, and then pedaled her way up to my ranch. My driveway alone would have eliminated most newbies. She remained committed rain or shine, and quickly found her way into my heart.

This woman was a natural with the horses. She was quiet, calm, listened, and took in all the equine nuances. She began to accompany me on some of my crazy journeys placing horses in sanctuary. We have made many memories together while travelling, working, fundraising, and getting to know one another. She is enormously valued and always a pleasure. I just love Sarah.

As Sarah graduates from university, she begins her journey in veterinary medicine. While we have many years of age that separate us, our hearts are closely aligned. She will be preparing for her future and remain tucked right here in my loving thoughts.

CHAPTER 14

Texas Secrets

In the early days of my horse rescue, I learned quickly to rely on my universe and my God. I believe nothing happens by accident and there are no coincidences—synchronicity, yes, but coincidence, no. As one can imagine, it is not an easy task. I have learned to look to the everyday clues to provide comfort and insight. Like I said, it isn't always easy but it always works out. So without hesitation, I agreed to take four mares with foals at their side. These horses were being hauled from Texas all the way to Fallon, Nevada. Why on earth would someone do that? I will explain.

Fallon, Nevada, has multiple feedlots, auction houses, and a culture of ranchers and cowboys qualified to throw down unequalled amounts of abuse and neglect. They work and ride their horses hard until, for them, their beasts become nothing more than a used up commodity. They dump them at the feedlot and repeat the cycle again. For obvious reasons I nicknamed Fallon, Nevada, "The Doorstep to Hell."

Back in 2007, the public outcry to shut down the slaughterhouses was in full force. The nation was aware and up in arms over the controversial slaughterhouses. As I have previously mentioned,

these foreign-owned houses "process" horsemeat for human consumption overseas. The general public was finally getting their way
and moving toward shutting them down. We don't eat horses in
America. We don't want our horses butchered. There was a nasty
little breeding barn in Texas feeling the heat.

Now, the Texas ranchers—big quarter horse breeders—who
owned these horses didn't want any attention. They didn't want any
controversy. They understand all to well that the quarter horse is
the number one horse in the nation going to slaughter. More quarter horses than any other breed end up butchered and served up on
foreign dinner plates. "Off the track" Thoroughbreds are runners
up. No matter, the AQHA doesn't want any parameters or restric-
tions on their breeding programs. The Thoroughbred breeders slip
the slow ones out the back door weekly to the "truck." Statistics
from 2016 indicate that over 140,000 American horses went to
slaughter in Mexico and Canada.

The Texans had a plan to sneak these eight horses out of Texas
and dump them in Nevada. Destroying their papers, and any connecting documentation that places them at this Texas ranch, was
the way it would go down. Their adoring public and all their valued
customers would never be the wiser. This would forever erase these
mares and their foals off the face of Mother Earth.

The Internet is a beautiful thing. The power of instant communication can transform a date with death to a date with destiny.
Once the news was out, we mobilized. The truck hauling the horses
to Fallon was intercepted by a Northern California horse rescue. An
equine version of "Let's Make a Deal" began on the side of the road
at a rest stop outside Fallon. The meat price per pound was estimated and paid. They offered the haulers a fair price. Kill haulers
are not loyal. He who holds the cash in hand wins. They were safe.
The mares and foals were loaded and brought to us.

The back area of my property had not yet been cleared or pre-pared for use. I only had my one little T-staked pasture erected. A foster pasture was needed to handle these new arrivals. Gracious friends welcomed the eight with loving enthusiasm. All eight horses arrived late in the afternoon and on one trailer.

Four mares with four foals at their side is a site to behold, each one more magnificent and graceful than the next. We all stood and watched them like kids in line at the carnival. Wide-eyed with anticipation, we gasped at their beauty. What is it about a horse that makes folks want to stare? My eyes can never seem to get their fill.

We had a bay mare with a little chestnut filly sticking close to her side. She would be Lena, and her filly we called Carmella. Although after getting to know her, we thought Carmella should have been Porsche. It fit better. She was flashy, opinionated and fast. Next, a stocky, old school, bulldog-type, strawberry roan unloaded. May. Her filly, Daisy, was a duplicate. When baby looks identical to mommy, we call them Mini-Mes. Third pair off was a thin, crabby, don't-touch-me type with her spunky colt bouncing at her flank. He looked like he was tie-dyed in a tub of brown, beige and black ink, and so he earned his name Ty. We called mom Shila.

A black, thick head poked out of the rear door. A white blaze marked the entire front of her face. I swear I thought there should have been a drum roll. She was stoic, quiet. Surveying the landscape with authority, this enormous mare began her descent. Her pres-ence was so great that I felt she was moving in slow motion. Her colt was questioning what was being asked. With a misguided plop, he landed on top of her hind flank and skidded to the ground. She never flinched. With a slight nod, she instructed him to hop up and move along. He regained his composure and moved on into the pasture. The cream-colored colt began with his head to the ground then, releasing his pent up energy, bucked continuously into the center of the pasture. Proud of himself, he stood and looked back toward his mother.

Stella slowly walked into the pasture area. I inhaled deeply as I took in the sight in front of me. Eight lives saved and eight new responsibilities upon my shoulders. I blinked and thought for a moment. It felt like I was hovering above them, my eyes gazing downward upon them in a protective gesture. They stood unconcerned and grazing happily. This instance of fear was washed away with an overwhelming feeling of love. I appreciated being able to stand and gaze upon this beauty. In this moment, I realized I was doing what I needed to do. All the scary voices inside me quieted. I stood and felt the breeze touch my cheek, and took in the familiar smell of horse. All would be well.

Stella moved deeper into the pasture and I noticed a small hesitation in her movement. Something wasn't right. It was tough to tell. It was an ever so slight favoring to the other front leg. Horses will go to great lengths to cover an injury. If the herd realizes that a member may be injured, it can put the entire herd in harms way. To be extricated from the herd, to be alone, could mean death. Predators are forever on the look out for an easy meal. This is how a horse's brain works. Survival first.

I spent a good portion of that afternoon sitting on the knoll above the pasture gate just watching the new group. My friends and the quiet husband packed up to head back to their busy workday one by one. I watched Stella. She began to keep an eye on me. She knew I was on to her. She dismissed me and moved away.

Morning brought a quiet Saturday. I was free to linger in the new herd. Every single mare was untouchable, and every foal following momma's lead. I walked about keeping my eyes down, observing the little details. As the foals began to feel comfortable and safe, they began to play. Biting, kicking, and rearing up on hind legs is great fun when you're 9 weeks old. I had to keep an eye on four rambunctious youngsters while trying to get close to Stella.

This stoic mare was hiding an injury. I could tell.

I approached her softly. I looked down and held my breath. She stood grazing and lifted her head about halfway, acknowledging my presence. Then she resumed eating. I was grateful for the enticing fresh grass. I approached her again, closer, my eyes fixed above and beyond her. She lifted her head and remained still. I could feel my heart beating in my chest. My ears were heavy, my pulse looking for a way to get out of my body. I was so close to this mare. Her neck was now inches from my face. The smell of her coat was full, rich and dusty. I leaned my cheek against her neck. I brushed her neck softly, not daring to lift a hand. She licked and chewed, in horse words it conveys we have spoken. I stood frozen now. I knew we had connected.

It would be the only time that Stella, this gracious and majestic mare, would ever connect with anyone. Little did I realize there was sadness yet to come. By afternoon her injury was more pronounced and the director of the Humane Society had arrived. Graciously, along with my vet, Dr. Natalie, we tried to dart and sedate this untouchable mare. I prayed we could take care of the sedation quickly so we could get in to take a look at her injury.

That was not to be.

It took over an hour and three darts shot from a gun to sedate this terrified mare. With a lump in my throat, I watched as she fought with every last bit of strength to stay standing. And then, like a heart broken from disappointment, she collapsed. I kept praying we could just get in, look at the leg, patch her up, and all would be well.

Again, that was not to be. Both vets had diagnosed a shattered shoulder.

"This cannot be fixed." I heard their words but couldn't move. I shook my head.

"She needs to be put to rest."

I couldn't bring myself to say the words. I had my left hand on her neck and could feel her warmth. I didn't comprehend what I was being told. I had a decision to make. It had to be made now.

"No chance?" I asked.

My voice wasn't my own. I heard a little girl inquiring about her beloved guinea pig. One last pitiful peek at a little cold body wrapped in a favorite washcloth and placed lovingly in a shoebox. Notes of love and flowers accompanied my little one to the other side. I felt the pit in my stomach. Stella would have no such dignity. Her end came unexpected, uninvited. Every bit of terror she felt was justified. She had been right. She was in grave danger. She wasn't going to ever get to wake up.

All the hopefulness of the day was now gone. I placed a washcloth over her eyes and prayed for it to be over. But again, that was not to be.

I sat on the grassy knoll and watched the vets drive away. They had done everything they could for this mare. Alone now, I sat.

Her little cream-colored colt appeared from the perimeter of my sorrow. He came and stood sentinel over his mothers' body. The tears soaked my face. His quiet posture stood alone. He lowered his head and just stood.

I was impatient, as the tallow company had not arrived. I had no options but to have her body carried away. It was not my land. I could not bury her here. This poor little guy had to stand and wait. It seemed unimaginable to me. The sorrow hung in the air.

I don't speak any Spanish and the man driving the tallow truck didn't speak any English. But with hands waving and gesturing it became understood that insurance and liability issues would not let him enter the pasture. In any language, I understood and was again mortified. As he shook his head "no," I mustered up the courage to get the mare out of the pasture.

I had to hog-tie her back feet and attach them by rope to my bumper. I could feel the weight of her lifeless body as I slowly pulled her up the hill and out to the other side of the fence. Now she lay there dust covered with portions of her once beautiful coat shredded and ripped. I watched as the chain pulled her up the ramp and into the body of the bin. My chest was burning with sadness. What a heinous ending for this mare. What an undignified end. I sat on the knoll and cried all the tears in my universe. My chest heaved and sighed until I had no strength. Exhausted, spent and feeling completely alone, I made an effort to go home. RIP, Stella, for a brief moment you were so loved.

"Lynn, how many horses you have at your place now?

"Nine dad, I have nine," I replied.

I pulled the casserole out of the oven and placed the hot pads on the counter.

"You can never get a straight answer from her can you, Peg?" My mother smiled, glancing as if she were responding to my dad for me.

"Isn't there some place you can send those horses? Isn't there an organization that will take them?" She inquired with no more interest than the casual curiosity of a visiting stranger.

"Well, no, mom, that would be me. It's what I do." I threw glances to the floor.

"Well, it's just a shame dear. They must cost you a fortune." She looked to my father for approval.

"I'm a real charity mom. People donate money for me to do my work."

"Well, you already have enough on your plate! Working full time, the children…why add the stress?"

"I love the horses, mom, I want to make a difference."

"Well you can't save them all." Her voice softened and I heard a mumbling. "It's just ridiculous. All of the running around you must do! Just ridiculous."

Dinner was served and the conversation continued. All I heard was, "Wha Wha Whawha Wha."

CHAPTER 15

The Mare with Four Foals

The phone call came in, "Can you take a mare with a foal?"

"Ah, yes, I have room." I replied and began to rearrange horses in my mind. *Who would fit where, and who got along in pasture with one another?* An hour later, the phone rang again.

"Apparently this palomino mare has adopted a second foal. She is nursing them both. Do you have the room?"

"Well, yes. It's OK, they can come." I rearranged once again in my head and created a place for mom plus two. The next couple of days the volunteers prepped the lower pasture for foals. The third phone call was placed and I had to chuckle.

"Are you kidding me?"

This mare now had pulled in three orphans and was nursing them along with her own. Shirley explained, "They are all bay foals, we can't tell them apart. She is loving them and treating them all equally."

Three babies, less than maybe 4 weeks old, had been ripped away from their panicked mothers. Then the mares were loaded onto the "Death Truck" for the horrific journey to the slaughterhouse.

Trembling and frightened, they stood clumped in a corner of the feedlot.

It was then a very small miracle occurred. The soft-eyed palomino mare quietly walked over and stood between the babies and the truck. She had her own foal at her side, which was now peeking around from the far side of her flank. The little ones could smell milk and smell mom. Usually a mare is very protective of her own foal, and of her own milk supply, so the three stood quietly hesitating. This mare gently nudged the babies closer to her side. For comfort, one nursed and jostled for position, and then nursed some more. Baby number two nudged in and took a turn, and then number three. This amazing mare adopted all three of these orphans as her own.

Upon their arrival, my daughter Jillian and I sat on the fence boards observing their behavior. The palomino mare seems content and pleased to be safe. The littles were not so sure. Fresh hay and water was available, yet the four stuck together.

Jillian hopped down off the fence board and quietly approached the tiny herd. She had her back to them, and crouched down ever so slightly. It must be the good kid energy. In unison, like a gaggle of baby ducklings, they crept toward her. One stretched his neck toward the back of her head. She decided to stay very low, almost sitting, and remained very still. In a moment's breath, she had four curious noses sniffing her head, inspecting her ears, and smelling her sweatshirt. I had to grin. Curiosity has its purpose.

It didn't take long and the babies began looking forward to our visits. We are supplementing the mare we have now named Angel. We provide formula four times a day. They all continue to nurse. They all continue to thrive.

Fast-forward by just one week. The day begins—up at 6 a.m.—and we check the milk buckets. *Yippee, they're empty!! The babies have* figured it out! When I would go into the pasture to feed, they'd begin to nicker and stand right behind me like little soldiers.

"Got Milk?"

Angel continued to take meticulous care of all her foals. As they grew and thrived, we gentled, vaccinated, and found them forever homes. Angel too has been adopted and lives close by in Watsonville. I see her occasionally and send her my love and appreciation. Her kindness was extraordinary and the fact she ended up almost sent to slaughter is unimaginable.

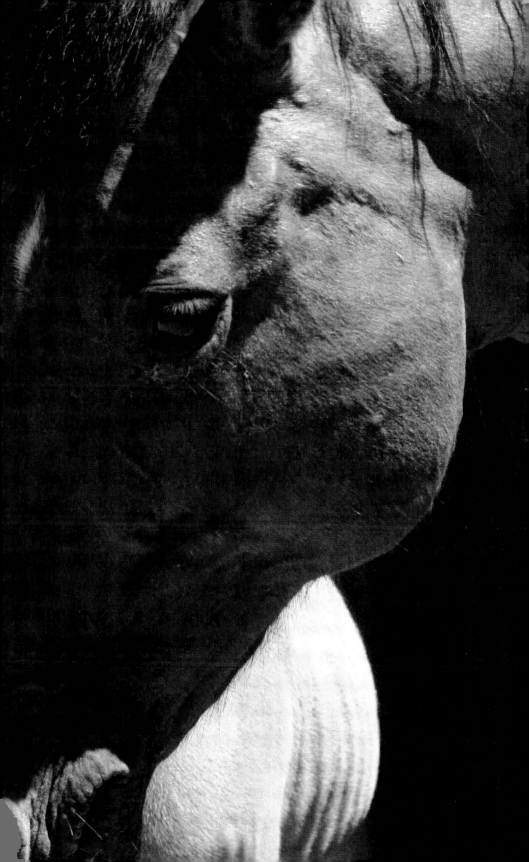

CHAPTER 16

My Dog Days At The Rescue

The days at the ranch seamlessly blended together with one following the next, and our experiences nourishing our relationship with Mother Nature. The chatter delivered by the chirping ground squirrels and scolding blue jays became daily conversations. The soft hooting of our great horned owls as they perched in the fragrant eucalyptus created my evening lullaby. I began to synchronize with my landscape. Manmade items like television, radio, and computers became less of a temptation and a bit of a nuisance. I didn't want to miss listening to the coyotes running or, perhaps, the braying of the neighbor's donkey at night because of these distractions. David enjoyed evenings in the garage tending to his workshop and tinkering away at his latest project. I tended to our brood—both two-and four-legged.

Surprisingly, not all the four-legged creatures living here are horses. Dogs have always been a huge part of my life and living on a ranch it became an irresistible temptation to have an entire pack. We arrived with two: Jake, a skinny hilarious Italian greyhound, and Shadow, the family golden retriever. Jake was the indoor dog and Shadow was the outdoor dog. Problem was that Jake had the worst potty habits known to man or beast. Jake lives to be warm. He would pretend to go to the door and then sneak around and make a beeline for the upstairs. Picture running all over the household— ah, that would be me running, not him—as it was not uncommon in order to keep Jake from having an accident. Really? Is it an accident when you purposefully won't go outside because it's too cold and so you sneak around a corner to piddle on my carpet? I think not! Shadow remained happily outside rolling in any kind of putrid smell he could discover.

Even though Italian greyhounds have Italian in the title don't be fooled. The name of the breed is only a reference to its popularity in Renaissance Italy. Italian greyhounds originated more than 4,000 years ago in the countries now known as Greece and Turkey. Small greyhound skeletons and depictions of them in early art support this theory. Little greyhound mummies have been discovered in Egypt. I can just imagine Jake lying around on a silk couch with Cleopatra.

"Another bite of sardine, my sweet adorable hound?"

"Yes, please, my queen."

One must always check a blanket or comforter before sitting down. Jake is predictably curled up under it. Unless of course there is a roaring fire, then he places his skinny little fanny right in front of the heat.

One of my, ahem, larger mistakes came about five years after our move to the ranch. In front of our local feed store was a box. Yes, that's right, a cardboard box. It had two Chihuahua puppies in it. Not sure where my senses went for just that moment, but home came one. Don't ask me why. I can't explain stupidity, especially my own. She was as cute as a puppy could possibly be. Sleeping long hours with her four limbs sticking straight up into the air and endearing us with every grunt, we named her Anna. The quiet husband named her "God dammit!"

Anna became the boss of the household. She bullied Jake at every pass. He could barely get in front of the fire anymore. We began calling her Anna-Moose. It just was a better fit. She gets in the trash, opens her own crate without permission, barks nonstop, tries to bite strangers, and generally disobeys any rules we put in place. I kept trying to rehome her, but people know better and steer clear. She now is known as Anna-Moose, worst dog in the world and lucky to be loved.

Shadow passed away from leukemia when he was 11 years old. It was horrible saying good-bye. I sat and stroked his beautiful red face until the light in his eyes dimmed. I'll never erase the image from my mind. I left the exam room and hugged my kids. Dave wrapped his big arms around all of us and we sobbed. There we stood, all of us, huddled in grief in the office reception area.

We mourned the loss of our beloved Shadow for many months. Being the mom, I presume I have this built in uncontrollable mechanism that has to fix everything for the family...*always*. Once again, I had a brilliant idea! I thought I'd fix the problem by bringing not one but two puppies home! What a splendid idea. A golden retriever we named Wyatt, and a chow and lab mix we named Bella. In a blink of an eye, we now had two huge grown outdoor dogs. Terrific. And it wasn't before too long that my big dogs made a bad choice. I'm not sure if they were bored or feeling neglected with so many horses around, but it happened. They decided to join a gang. Really. And I have proof!

Coyotes run and they howl in the deepest part of the night. It's not uncommon to lay in the dark and listen to the echo of their howls as it bounces off the valley walls. It was about 10 a.m. when my neighbor from two driveways over strolled up my driveway with a kind smile and a sad story. Lamberto explained that my dogs had scaled his 5-foot fence and took out six baby goats. Six? Did I hear that correctly?

"Where were the coyotes?" I sheepishly inquired.

"No coyotes. Just your big black dog and this one." He pointed to Wyatt. Wyatt looked away. He added, "This one sat on the outside trying to get in."

"Swell," I mumbled.

"I'm sure I heard coyotes last night. No coyotes?" I repeated the question. Lamberto shook his head. Isn't that just like a group of bad guys making the newbies take the heat? Geesh. Bad Luck. What bad luck! *Damn coyotes*, I was thinking to myself.

"How much?" I raised my eyebrows grimacing.

"$100 each."

Oh, my God, you stupid dogs! I couldn't believe my bad fortune. I promised Lamberto I would make good on my debt and stood a poorer person watching as he drove out of sight. However, the day was not done.

The white van with a friendly dog and little kitten on the side is not the van one looks forward to seeing heading up your driveway.

Animal Control rolled up, and before the officer could speak or finish closing his door, I blurted out, "Yeah, I know." I was chagrined. "I owe money now".

The animal control officer proceeded to tell me that each dog was not licensed and, in addition to the citation, I would have to pay a licensing fee. And, to add to my misery, my dogs would have to live on a chain the rest of their days, as we are not completely fenced.

"Are you serious?" I couldn't believe what I was hearing.

"Very," he replied.

Just then, with the most perfect timing, Anna–Moose bolts out the front door and begins attacking the officer's boot. Barking and growling, with all of her 6 pounds, she was relentless.

He glanced down and said, "I see she isn't wearing tags either. Is she licensed?" *That would be a NO!*

"No," I sheepishly replied.

Three citations and some $600 and something later, my day was done. Why did I need ranch dogs? Aren't little birds in the treetops enough company? I'm still trying to figure out that one.

It was very clear that there was no way I would subject my dogs to life at the end of a chain. Rehoming was the only option. It took a little doing, and a lot of tears, but both dogs made a lovely step up in life into their new homes. They both became inside dogs with fulltime companions.

It was a sunny afternoon and I was standing in front of the feed store working a recycling event for the rescue. A gorgeous new Ford truck pulled up to the drop-off space. I tried not to drool as I took in the glossy maroon and beige two-toned paint, the four-door carriage, and shiny rims. What a gorgeous truck. Smiling, I thought to myself, *I would be on vacation hauling horses with a rig like that.* I glanced up to the passenger seat and connected with a pair of deep brown eyes. A lion's mane of black fur framed the muzzle. The ears perked in curiosity. When the driver's door opened, this beguiling creature disappeared to make her exit. Bella! Leaning into hugs and smooches, I laughed at the site of this happy girl. She paused to check on her new guy and then resumed her celebration. She looked wonderful.

"She's the best dog I have ever known," he confirmed. "Sweet, obedient, goes everywhere with me. I thought you might like to say hello."

My heart was full. To witness her happiness and health sealed my decision that to rehome her was much better than sitting around waiting for me to get home. I profusely thanked him for taking the time to make this gesture. It meant so much to me.

I would learn about a year later that Wyatt, while not in as luxurious digs as Bella, was thriving nonetheless. His new man worked construction and the back of his truck was Wyatt Land. With the tailgate down, Wyatt went to work every morning and hung around while the day passed. Fresh water on the tailgate, a bed, toys, and treats took care of Monday through Friday. Day hikes filled the weekends. I am certain they are happy. I miss them, but know in my heart I did the right thing.

Often times I wonder if my animals realize they are supposed to behave like, well, the animals they are. My dogs behaved like wolves, and my horses often act like rambunctious little boys on the loose! Once more, I digress.

Whiskey and a gorgeous quarter horse, Dually (also known as Fatbutt) were the ranch clowns for a long period of time. Fatbutt is the affectionate nickname I gave Dually due to the sheer size of his fanny. He is a quarter horse after all. Their rumps are huge and for good purpose; they are the fastest horse on Earth running a quarter of a mile. It takes a big rumpus to make that happen! Dually was supposed to be my riding horse, but he always came up lame after the lightest ride. He was a fabulous horse with a great disposition but unfortunately suffered from a chronic lameness issue originating in his rear high hip area. Chiropractic sessions, equine massage, and even pills for inflammation had never provided lasting relief for Dually.

The afternoon was lazy and long. Jillian and I were busy in the house. A phone call came in asking if we were missing any horses.

"Uh, I don't think so. Let me check." I asked the caller to hang on.

I headed to the back area. The paddock door stood wide open, and the door next to it. Culprits! I thought to myself. Now what are they up to?

"Actually, I am missing two geldings! Geesh. Are they with you?"

"Well, not exactly. I mean they were with us." The caller went on to explain. "They were visiting on the fence with my mares, but as soon as they spotted us they took off."

I thanked the caller and Jillian and I headed out to go find our boys. Lead ropes and halters in hand, we began to walk the roads to see if we could locate them.

It wasn't but five minutes and voila. Their heads were in the grass, as an open meadow was enticing and available. We began walking in their direction. Whiskey lifted his head and, upon spotting us, sprinted in the opposite direction. Dually pulled his head up and was right on his heels. Hmm, I thought, *you're moving pretty good to me.* I stood wondering how that big rump could move so fast without a limp. We could almost hear them screaming with delight like naughty boys as they hightailed it across the meadow and down along yet another fence line. By now they had riled up all the horses in the neighborhood. They were all running along the fences, neighing and calling out. Well, doesn't this make for nice neighborly relations?

Jillian and I rolled our eyes and continued to hunt them down. Another 20 minutes passed and once again we found them grazing in a meadow of tall grass. *Come on boys, game times up.* Whiskey lifted his head again and began to saunter away from us. He approached a tree and proceeded to move around to the back of it. He took a quick peek and then hid his face behind the tree trunk—not his body, but just his face. He stood perfectly still.

We stood a moment and waited. He remained perfectly still.

"Mom, look," Jillian whispered, "he's hiding."

"You have got to be joking," I muttered. "He can't be serious?"

Jillian and I stood there and watched. Whiskey stood still as if the rest of his body that stuck out from behind the tree was somehow invisible. Neither a swish of his tail nor the sound of his breath was going to give him away.

"Don't laugh," I murmured. "He'll get mad and take off again."

By now Dually was completely confused as to what his role in this charade might be. He had stopped eating and was watching Whiskey. I imagine then he must have caught on because he began acting as though he wasn't looking at Whiskey. He began grazing in the opposite direction. He took a few casual steps carefully avoiding eye contact.

Do I look or not? He was struggling with the question. Jillian and I were trying not to make any noise, but shaking our heads in amusement. We wanted to bust out giggling like little girls. Then, it was momentous. Dually made an executive decision and decided to make a move. He went over and stood by Whiskey.

Aughh! For the love of Mike! Really? Whisk was none too happy with Dually. His wheels were spinning.

What are you doing? My cover is blown. Way to go, Fatbutt.

With halters and lead ropes on, we walked the boys toward home. Whiskey pouted the entire walk home, all the while shoulder checking Dually to run him off the grass whenever possible. Oh, the antics of naughty boys.

As we strolled over the landscape heading for home, Jillian decided to confide a bit of her personal social life with me. Her latest crush was showing interest and she was pleased and looking forward to school. I remained quiet, knowing that one wrong response could shut down the entire conversation. We parents know (or at least hope) these tidbits of information shared can shed great insight for improved parenting relations. I keenly and ever so quietly listened as she spoke.

"So, I'm thinking he may be getting ready to ask me to hang out."

I thought to myself, *what exactly is hanging out these days?* Is that dating, or being in a group, or going steady. Who says "going steady" anymore? I'm pretty sure I know what it doesn't mean. It had better not anyway. I've decided that current lingo is very hard to keep up with.

What I have learned is that if someone is chill, they are not cold. This means they are cool…you know, popular. If they are sick, they are not really sick or ill. That also means they are cool. If something is sick, well, that's even better. If you are lame you can still walk, but everyone thinks you are a socially awkward. "Whatever" is usually translated as "I'm pretty much done communicating now, could you go away?"

It never will cease to astonish me the things we do for our teenagers. Truth be told, I enjoy my kids very much. I like the casual, no-slack way they keep me young. I am no longer "up to it," but "down to go." I am not "overhearing gossip" but heard someone "talking all kinds." I am not "interested in something." Instead, I'm "all about that." My grandpa used to say, "youth is wasted on the young!" But in my kids and their friends I see nothing wasted. All I see is originality, humor, an honesty that I admire, and a confidence you cannot buy. These kids are our ambassadors for tomorrow and I am thrilled.

This all leads me to being thankful for our four-legged friends that don't share our language. No lingo, vernacular, or hip statements to keep up with. They don't remind us of our age, or our lameness (that's a word worse than "wrinkles" to an equine), or the fact that no one is looking at us anyway. I am certain they do communicate, both graciously and honestly, which to me is totally sick!

When Jillian asked if I wanted to go riding I responded with an enthusiastic "Yes!" How lovely I thought it would be just a little quiet time for my girl and me.

What I came away with is a lot of advice on how to stay sane. The first and most important thing to do is to get rid of your teenagers. Really send them away. Pack them up along with the smelly shoes and off they go. There can be nothing more infuriating than the realization that this person who once used to look up to you and admire you is now irritated with everything about you!

We decided to go for a quick ride on the nearby trails that take a rider up to the ridge for beautiful views. It was to be a simple bareback, easygoing walk-trot. I am still working on perfecting the sitting trot. Apparently this is not something I should be doing while in her presence. I realized a lot of what adults do embarrasses teenagers. OK, everything adults do embarrasses teenagers.

My daughter sat there on Whiskey (who is always perfect for her) impatiently waiting for me to get up on my horse. This small task was to be done from the ground, and without stirrups. She sat comfortably, only one ear available as the other was plugged into her iPod, She had one hand busy texting and receiving messages from her cell. She glanced up occasionally to see me struggling with mounting from the ground. With no assistance offered, I reassured myself, I could handle this. *I know what to do.* I went over to the fence to hop on. Leo moved away. I got off the fence, walked back around to the other side. I pushed him back to the fence, and went back around again and climbed up on the fence. He then moved away just in time for me to slip between him and the fence (thank you, Leo). I tried the third time and landed on his back and glanced up to see the eyes rolling in her head as if to say, "God, could you take any longer?"

I said, "What?" As in, "What are you looking at? What are you so impatient about? What is your problem young lady?"

She rattled off something about one of her friends who was going to hook up with so-and-so, and how lame, and he's a pig, and wait until school. Blah, blah, blah. It was then I thought, *It's not even about me. I could have landed face first in mud, or hung upside down under his belly backwards with both legs crisscrossed on his neck. She wouldn't have even noticed. Cause' it's about her.*

She said, "Ready mom?"

Oh yes, I thought, I am ready. Ready to find someone my own age to ride with!

It wasn't until about four years later that we both realized what a nice relationship a mother and daughter can hold. I had landed a job about a mile from the ranch. It was a joy not ever having to hop on a freeway for weeks at a time. I used to share a car with Jillian and it just happened that she had school on my birthday. I got a text about 4:30 pm telling me she was there to pick me up. I gathered my belongings and headed out the front door.

To my surprise, there sat Jillian on Whiskey, and Sarina, Jillian's pal, on her horse Lion. Leo was in a rope halter. I smiled. What a sweet surprise.

Word spread faster than fire and my entire department clamored outside to ooh and aah over these magnificent animals. They stood quietly as if being the center of attention was written in their job description. After much appreciation and ego stroking, the horses seemed ready to depart. We lazily headed down the road and out of sight. It was a moment for me to appreciate the smallest things. My daughter's thoughtfulness touched my heart. My horses warm my thoughts and make me smile.

"It's not bad to get a year older when you celebrate it like this!"

CHAPTER 17

How Does One Define Grief?

Six years in and the Pregnant Mare Rescue was now nationally networked. Facebook, newsletters, media interviews, and word of mouth had successfully put us on the map. Once again the call came in to help pregnant mares out of Canada. We raised $10,000 to pay the ransom and haul. We'd commit to three and rescue four. I am overwhelmed that, as they arrive at my little rescue, they show me kindness. A small quiet nicker welcomes me. It translates directly to my heart as, "Could there be hope? Am I really safe?"

One liver chestnut mare, Petal, was horribly thin and eating my dirt. We had left bundles of fresh grass hay out for an all night feast. By sunrise not a trace was to be found. These four mares were starving! I have no proof and I have no evidence, but they look to me as though they had been fending for themselves in the Canadian or North Dakota cold, perhaps knee deep in snow for many months.

Day three and the four mares are happily welcoming the ongoing feast. They have access to fresh grass hay all day and I supplement their lunch with some rice bran and sweet grain. It is so tempting for them that I actually trade touching for treats. You smell and touch my hand then you get a bite to eat. I stroke your face and you get the bucket. Boy, they learn fast.

Another mare, Malibu, wants none of it. I was told that this mare stood on a Premarin line for almost 10 years. Her first nine foals were sent off to slaughter. Her last baby, Madrid, was born here with us. Malibu's pretty face still reflects the pain, sadness, and the inexplicable grief of living in a barn of 80 mares all suffering the same loss. Babies sent to slaughter—Horse Auschwitz. I am pleased to have been able to get Malibu to a better circumstance. She has nice digs, fresh water, her new foal at her side, and an abundance of hay. Yet some days she stands with tears in her eyes. Are there enough days left in her life to undo her pain and suffering? I don't know. What I do know is that she is forever in our care, forever under our protection. She will never have another horrific experience.

This estrogen industry is a clever evil entity. Regulation and perhaps a conscious are not items in demand. With Canadian pressure for regulation and change, the industry is simply moving on. They are taking their horror and going to a country where the blood bath can continue without rules, without regulation. China waits with open arms.

It is a tough lesson in reality and disappointment. Like it or not, even with your very best effort put forth, sometimes circumstances just don't go the way one had hoped. Frustration, anger, and a sense of hopelessness can often settle in. I feel the same way about the mental condition of my mom. I miss having real conversations with her. The vacancy in her voice tells me she doesn't remember from day to day what she's done, where she has been.

I call to check in and we talk about the weather. I think to myself, *here is the woman who raised me, who knows more about me, my life than any other person on the planet, and we are talking about nothing.*

She has been a constant provider of love, a constant in my life. Yet, when we talk over the phone, it's her voice but it's not really her. I ask the same questions and she gives the same answers. She asks about the kids but as time passes she is a little more hesitant to ask. I wonder if she worries about repeating herself.

It is enormously painful, the emptiness inside. Her sense of humor is not present. Her wisecrack remarks are gone. I feel a part of me can now exhale from the pressures everyone feels from their mother. But so much of my mother is gone. My dad tends to her needs and keeps a close eye on his partner of more than 67 years.

Death arrives in many ways. Some pass very quickly. Some die tragically. Others, it would seem, die slowly and so it is sad to watch. It creates a gaping hole in the heart. I am watching my mother die. I don't remember exactly when it became so hard. I wonder too if I am watching Malibu slowly die. As I feel it now, I get lost in my own grief.

CHAPTER 18

My Divine Protection

do believe Divine Protection is everywhere. I have to remind myself often when my days are hard. And my days can get very hard.

CHAPTER 19

Driving Miss Daisy

met her on Monday. I stood quietly and stared in complete disbelief. The pain and suffering inflicted upon this lovely mare is nearly indescribable. My heart sank. My girlfriend cried all night and I simply could not ignore this mare. Daisy needed help and I was determined to be the one. I joined forces with my friends, Kendra and Frances. We scrambled to put together a decent bribe. We were told he was keeping her alive just for the baby. Our determination steadied. We made a reasonable offer and paid half up front. It's difficult doing business with the devil.

On the next visit, Frances shared with this mare that she would be leaving soon. Frances slipped the horse some pain medication and explained that it would be morning before she could pick her up. She stood brushing the dead hair off her emaciated body. The owner showed up with another person and this mare hobbled in agony to the far end of the shelter. She retreated to the furthest corner of her stall and our hearts broke all over again. Frances made a silent promise to her. "I will come get you."

Morning found that horse standing alert at the stall door. She was about to escape from the gates of hell. She was about to be set free. She wore shoes, which had probably been on her hooves longer than four or five years. Her hooves appeared 8 inches too long, and her front legs trembled under her weight as she moved forward. Sweating and working as hard as she could, that mare walked to the trailer and stepped up. She and Frances never looked back.

The relief and gratitude this mare displayed will touch your heart. How do you stay so sweet when you are subjected to such abuse? Her front teeth were chipped and broken off. I guesstimate her overall Henneke score for health and body condition must be about a 2. Her body wheezed when she sighed, and a cough may suggest worm infestation.

I was told it was suspected she was a victim of "horse tripping." Remember we talked about blatant horse abuse? Our work had just begun. She was now comfortable in her own stall. Eight inches of fresh, deep shavings will keep any more bedsores at bay. Mike, a wonderful farrier, came out on a moment's notice and took off the shoes. He trimmed up what came off easily. Under the glaring lights of portable electricity, she stood quietly leaning into Cassidy, another wonderful farrier, while the years of abuse were clipped away. Tears on every face were proof enough that the right decision had been made. We massaged her sore limbs, administered pain relief, and made sure she had continuous fresh hay and water.

Dr. Terry arrived in the morning to assess the situation. Kendra showed up with a little waif of a child, about 7 years old. Kendra told me this child speaks to angels. She also speaks to animals. The doctor of veterinary medicine met the child communicator. Two worlds stood side by side. Graciously, they each made their assessments.

Dr. Terry said this poor mare was in a lot of discomfort. Lungs had fluid, temperature was high, tendons were strained, and hooves were horrendous. Her age was estimated at 25-plus years. The final diagnosis was pneumonia with a body score of just 1.5. Euthanasia was suggested.

Then the little girl entered the stall and sat closely. She tucked her skirt under her legs and leaned forward, eyes closed. Her tiny hands touched Daisy's neck and then slowly stroked her check.

She whispered, "I understand." After but a moment she glanced up at the adults,

"She is worried about her unborn foal. She lives only to see her birth".

Dr. Terry explained that she could not successfully bring a baby into the world in her condition.

Nodding, the little voice replied, "Yes, I will tell her."

Complete disbelief engulfed me as this small collection of adults stood quietly taking in the conversation between this child and Daisy. Silent glances were exchanged.

Who told her she might be pregnant? Where did this little body get such an old soul? Am I the only one standing in complete shock? My questioning thoughts were interrupted.

"She is ready to go," affirmed the little girl as she came to a stand.

Daisy heaved her body forward and backward then up she stood. The little girl reached up and opened the stall door. They made a quiet exit. Her tiny hand never left the mares shoulder. Side by side and up to the grassy area, they walked with no lead line or halter. We all stood frozen, watching this little angel at work. Guiding a weary soul to the other side is no small task. She made it look effortless. And with all the graciousness one would imagine for an angel to display, she helped that mare lay down.

Settled in and lying comfortably in tall grass, the little girl announced, "She is ready now. She understands she will have new feet, a better body and no more pain. She is looking forward to seeing her baby."

Daisy crossed over quietly and peacefully.

The little girl smiled and said with such love, "There, she is much better now. God bless you, Daisy, God bless your little one".

Kendra, with her psychic abilities that make me believe she is from an alternate dimension anyway, began talking and brought everyone back from our frozen observations. Again I could feel the breeze upon my cheek, and hear the sounds of the raptors fussing in the trees. Leaves rustled once again. I felt as though the earth was breathing again, releasing a big exhale, as yet another soul had crossed.

What just transpired here? My thoughts were quieted by the overwhelming comfort of knowing.

It sends me into the hallowed, quiet space of church. It brings my mother's face to light. She is there—young, smiling, caring for, and watching over us. I kneel with hands folded in prayer. I feel a light peering through colorful stained glass. The stream of light impairs my vision, yet I feel that I am seeing so clearly. I see my father as a young parent. My little brother listens as it's explained to him that this is really where the golf course begins. With talent beyond his age, he soaks in the opportunity to stand on the edge of the Earth and play—to stand on the silky grass next to greatness. The coastal salt air permeates their surroundings. The ocean roars as the wind swirls up froth from the tide. The view is extravagant. It is a moment inside a bigger moment called life.

I hear the waves thrash up onto the sand. I feel the air in my nose and the tears sitting on my face. I am transported to many places instantly—to all places at once. It is profound to feel connected to all. We really are all one. I breathe, you fly, and one will snort and trot. We stand reaching upward to the heaven. We hope for the life where form does not exist, where healing is complete, and where pain is non-existent. We are all one in love and peace.

CHAPTER 20

The Paiutes

The Paiute (PY-yoot) tribe is actually many different bands distributed across a large part of the western United States. I received word that large groups of Paiute mustangs from a Native American reservation in northern Nevada were being culled from their herd. It had grown too large, and the chief had been assured that they would be adopted into homes from the Fallon Feedlot. We believed differently, and the call came to those that could help to rescue the 200 horses.

The community mobilized. The first group of people took on the task of raising the ransom. A second group took on the task to find layover. Once removed and saved, the horses would need a safe place to go and might spend up to a week waiting for a rescue pick up.

A third group began sending out the word. My connection informed me that they had already counted 20, all less than 16 weeks of age and now orphaned. I didn't have to ask what had happened to their mothers.

I arrived at the Shiloh Foundation in Lincoln, California, to claim my four. They huddled together at the far end of their corral.

Stealing glances over each other's flanks, they leaned into each other for security. The babies were a mere 24 hours out from being ripped away from their mothers.

There they stood. Fannies facing me as if to say "Go away, leave us alone!" I understood and tried to make their transition as easy as possible. I moved slow and as non-threateningly as possible. They were scared but amazingly reasonable. They popped in, and with the doors closed they began their journey to safety. We made sure to stop and do checks. Peeking in the trailer window I looked down upon four little heads. One foal was lying down. The rest stood. No one bothered to look up. The trip would be quiet. They stood still. Occasionally one would nibble a bit of grass from the floor. Mostly they just stood. Little did they realize that fate had smiled upon them. They had been spared that horrific death.

Our arrival after nightfall was uneventful. It was the following morning as I made my way down to their pasture that we all met. The unwelcoming glances continued. They looked at me with utter confusion on their little faces.

"What do you want?"

I sat down with alfalfa on my lap. Hmmm…ears pricked. I sat and waited, looking the other way. Many moments passed and then there was a step. One foal, the only colt, leaned his head forward and took another step. He stretched his neck as long as he possibly could, all the while keeping his eye on me. He made the decision. He stepped again and took a mouthful, retreating so quickly that he dropped most of his prize onto the dirt. He crunched and stood, eyes focused on me. The other three observed intently, but did not dare make a move.

The little colt moved forward slowly but steadily into love and kindness. He would be full of firsts: first to be touched, first to allow scratches to his neck. The fillies followed his lead. Courage to address the unknown is a gift. And to hold enough curiosity in your heart and smarts in your head puts courage in motion. I cannot think of anything braver than a soldier. And so befitting, I called him Soldier. His journey in his life had just begun. He held all the promise and hope that I carry in my own heart for every horse in the nation.

Imagine a morning in the pasture where the sun has finally returned and I am all ready to put my best foot forward. I was ready for the day! I worked my way down to the Paiutes: Faith, Sapphire, Soldier and Sunny. At first I didn't see anyone. Then a nostril popped up, followed by an eyeball peering over the fence boards from inside the shelter.

"Good morning," I said. I hear several nickers but can only see one head. It's Faith. She's the only one tall enough to peek over the paddock boards. I have been spending time in the pasture with the foals and so this morning my goal is to begin doing haltered walk'abouts inside the corral. The herd of four looks at me like I've lost my mind. My silly made-up anthropomorphic conversation begins in my head.

"What is that in her hand?"

"A predator, what else?"

"Why on earth is she walking him around with that thing by his face?"

"I think it's called a hauler."

"No! It's a halter."

"I dunno what it is, glad it's not me."

"Well, He is getting an apple from her."

"Really? Let's go follow…Wait, what's an apple?"

They all line up and begin to walk behind me. Funniest thing I've ever seen. I am the Pied Piper with an apple in hand. The scent is so enticing, they cannot resist. I walk around and then stand, and begin to position myself at the side. I place a quiet hand on the rump of an unsuspecting foal. Pop! The rump goes up and then down. My hand is still there. Now this little girl, Sapphire, has to decide if it's worth leaving the treat to get away from my hand. She decides "no" and continues eating her sweet treat.

The remaining three shoot glances of indignation at me. Just who do I think I am? I'm the food lady, that's who. I stroll away and then they follow. By the day's end, and four sessions of about a half-hour each, I am touching all the foal fannies.

An opportunity presented itself and I had a decision to make. A very well-known, popular horse whisperer had offered to take my four orphans and further their gentling along. They were pocket ponies right about now, just days from haltering. I thought, *Wow! I have been chosen. This could be terrific.*

I managed to load them up sans any trauma and we hit the road. So far, I calculated, they had loaded from the feedlot to the Shiloh foundation, from Shiloh to the ranch, and now they have loaded again without incident. This was very, very good as bad experiences are huge when they are so young. A bad experience could imprint them for a lifetime. I was so pleased they were coming along so nicely. I was promised that they would be ready to come home in six weeks, vaccinated, haltering and leading. Sounds great, I thought, I'm in.

It's a disappointing moment when you feel you've been duped. It's a tragic moment when you feel what has transpired might not be able to be undone. I went to pick up two of the four, as Faith and Soldier had been adopted together and were now in their new home.

What I found upon my arrival would make you cry. My babies were freaked out, nervous, and frightened. Loading them to haul home wasn't good and our arrival back at the ranch was worse. For the millionth time, I had to ask to borrow my neighbor's pasture because I could pull the trailer right into it. There I could open the door and they'd hop out into a safe pasture. Then I could push them up through the dividing gate and into my pasture. *So much for haltering and leading,* I thought. I couldn't even touch them. What or who had pushed them over their threshold?

I was enormously disappointed to state the obvious. They were used as a commodity for the benefit of the students. It was supposed to be the other way around. The talents of the trainer and his students were supposed to be there for the rescued babies. I am here for my horses—to help them. They were not to go somewhere to be used as objects while students learned the right and/or wrong ways to handle a horse. In short, I was furious.

All the gentling had been undone and, as any horse person knows, all the damage that had been done will now be life long. My easygoing, trusting foals will forever be suspicious and wary. Yes, they will come along and make great strides. But I make no mistake when fully understanding that the damage is done. While months later a sweet man adopted both of them, it was short lived. In less than a year's time I was heading up to El Sobrante, California, to once again reclaim my little foals.

The following is the story told according to my dear friend and hauler extraordinaire, Donna:

It's Lynn's policy that a horse can always come back, so she gave me a call and we went up to get the fillies. She posted on her blog about it and Laurie Dearinger, founder of the newly formed Blue Horse Rescue, read the blog and offered to take one of the mares, Sapphire, as her first rescue! So our mission was to go to Alberto's, in El Sobrante, pick up both mares, take Sapphire up to Laurie's place near Santa Rosa, then bring Sunny home to Larkin Valley.

Whew—a long haul for Lynn and I, but it would be epic for little Sunny.

I picked up Lynn at 7 a.m. and she told me Alberto had called to say that Sapphire had jumped out of her paddock and joined a herd of eight other horses in a "really large" pasture above his barn. Why would she jump out of her paddock? I would learn later he had separated Sunny and Sapphire. They way he executed this task, and his reasons for doing so, I will never understand. Sapphire had lost some ground since leaving Lynn's place and no longer dealt gracefully with a halter, so there were a bunch of things that made the situation complicated. Lynn was a little stressed.

Anyhow, we got there about 10 a.m. Alberto wasn't around so Lynn's first order of business was to check in with Sunny. By the time Sunny and Lynn were getting comfortable, Alberto arrived from the pasture where Sapphire was roaming. Alberto told us that his strategy was to halter the lead mare of the herd and just lead the whole bunch down to his area, then get Sapphire loaded into the trailer and lead the rest all back to the pasture. Lynn approved of the approach, but the problem was that Alberto and his two friends had had no luck catching the lead mare—and they'd been working at it since 7 a.m. We piled into Alberto's truck and went up to the pasture. Sheesh.

The pasture I keep my horse in is about 12 acres. Alberto's pasture is at least 150 acres. It has streams, trees, ridges, and several meadows. Alberto's two friends were on horseback in hopes they could get up on the ridge tops. From there the plan was to find the horses, and then sort of drive them in a general direction. But they couldn't get close enough to actually get a hand on that lead mare. One of the fellows was a roper and was using his lariat to drive the horses.

Lynn listened and watched for about two minutes and then took off walking down to the meadow nearest the gate. She had the mounted guys move the horses down to the meadow, then retreat to the ridge top. She just stood there for a few seconds, and then started slowly making her way into the nine-horse herd, keeping a really relaxed posture while avoiding eye contact with any of the horses. She got to the lead mare and squatted next to her. Pretty soon the mare put down her head. I don't know what Lynn did then, but she soon after stood up with her arms around the mare's neck and got Alberto to bring her a rope. Lynn tied a quick halter out of the rope and started leading the mare out, with the rest of the horses following!

The horses broke away several times, but Lynn and her "partner" mare just stood and waited while the caballeros got the horses back behind the mare to continue walking. About 20 minutes after we arrived, we were already back at Alberto's barn with Sapphire and Sunny in the arena and my trailer backed up to the gate. Lynn hadn't even looked at Sapphire while she was doing the "capture," so her first agenda item was to get to be friendly with her—via some alfalfa. Sapphire was all over that. Over the next 20 minutes, we got Sunny into the trailer—she's now good in a halter—and Sapphire followed her in without a halter.

The trust those mares put in Lynn—and, I guess, in each other—is miraculous. Sapphire, in particular, had spent the last three hours being chased by people on horseback, and an hour later she's stepping into a trailer like she's a Grand Prix horse who lives in a trailer! They settled in immediately. I had split up a flake of alfalfa and distributed it on the trailer floor (I don't think Alberto's rations ran to alfalfa) and we headed for Santa Rosa to Sapphire's new digs. Our epic journey ended on a good note. Sapphire was happily grazing in her new digs and Sunny was content to be back at the rescue. Lynn and I congratulated ourselves on a job well done. It was a long but safe day. The horses were delivered safely and all ended well.

Another six months passed and Laurie asked if she could also take Sunny. The trauma each filly had experienced was from the same circumstance, and Laurie felt she was up to the task of rehabilitation for our two girls. Donna, Sunny and I planned an early morning jaunt back up to Blue Horse.

Hot morning coffee in hand, we headed out. Enter *Captain's Log: Adventure One Million Forty-Four.* Rain was forecasted to be on the way and so we prepared to travel very safely. I was in full navigation mode, using Donna's fancy cellphone to check out the weather radar. It mentioned that the storm was closing in and it was about to get…heavy. *Heavy?* That is precisely the wrong word. A torrential downpour is what occurred! Employing the trusty cellphone once again, we located the next closest Starbucks and parked. Thank God we weren't moving. The rain descended upon us, the sky darkened, and I watched our visibility rapidly diminish from fair to bleak. I tried looking out the passenger window through streams of water only to see a river rising in the parking lot. The landscape was instantly brushed gray. I felt like I was immersed in a watercolor portrait. Customers were ankle deep, clamoring to get to the dry warm coffee shop. The blurred images disappeared inside. We sat and waited. The ping-ping of pelting water increased. I checked the cellphone once again. While the sound of rain hammering the truck cab was deafening, huge droplets splashed across the windshield in a sideways attack. The radar emanating from the little cellphone showed we were sitting exactly under the storm.

My thoughts ran to poor little Sunny out in the trailer. My logical, rational mind understood she was absolutely fine. But, as a mom, I was worried about the noise on the trailer roof. I didn't want her frightened. The last time I experienced this kind of deluge, I was about 8 years old. I got to ride inside the car while my mom and I went through the carwash. I was silenced with complete amazement as the machines, soap, and brushes all went to work scrubbing and rinsing. What fun! I remember pressing my nose against the glass to feel the cool window on my cheek and check for vibrations.

The water was relentless and I decided Sunny was, after all, a horse, and probably just fine. No need to take on unnecessary heroics. Sitting soaked for the remainder of our journey was not on my list of priorities. I would wait it out.

It seemed that just as soon as it had arrived and soaked into the earth, the fickle wind picked up and blew off the storm. Clear skies appeared and in another few moments we were pulling back out onto the highway. I made a mental note to appreciate coastal California weather. It's like Hawaii without the humidity.

Not a peep from little Sunny. A quick peek revealed her napping, standing comfortably in her shavings.

Upon our arrival, Laurie greeted us with a mug of warm coffee and squares of chocolate. There has never been a more gracious host—or gracious receiver of rescued horses. Laurie and I go back a few years and have become wonderful friends. I just love the kind of friend who is always glad to hear from you, never mind if you have forgotten her birthday and don't send out Christmas cards. She is just the nicest, kindest woman and I feel very blessed to have her as a friend.

Laurie and I met one summer when she registered to be a vendor at one of our fundraisers. She arrived, unloaded her goods, and we chatted as she set up her booth. She was darling in her denim skirt and peasant blouse. With a very stylish haircut and streaks of gray, she looked confident and smart. I made a mental note to try and be a bit more fashionable. We horsewomen have a tendency to let that slide. It's not often you're going to spot manicured nails and attractive jewelry on someone walking a horse. I kept thinking she looked so pretty and it all appeared so effortless.

We became good friends and her visits to the ranch became more frequent. Laurie would eventually fall in love with one of my babies, adopt him, and start her own rescue. Her little colt—scraggly, wormy, ribby, and snotty-nosed—was shy and oh so quiet. He would be called Patriot, or just P for short.

The backstory of Patriot is a touching tale of woe, disbelief, and a very happy ending. Upon his arrival, P was the messiest, poorest sight of a foal I have ever laid eyes on. His swollen ankles made standing difficult and so it was decided we would just sit. He arrived with an enormous palomino draft mare. She was acting as his surrogate, and was probably the reason why this little soul was still alive. She stood standing sentinel over both of us as P and I began our conversation.

I explained that, if he could hang on, things might just be OK for him. He was recovering from "strangles," a serious illness in horses resembling the human flu virus. He was very weak. X-rays revealed problems with both of his hind legs: a hairline fracture on the left, a bone chip on the right. I'm guessing a trailer door, or perhaps a large heavy gate, had slammed into his backend causing injury to his fragile legs. Who would do that to a baby? I promised I would take good care of him and that the worst was over. I looked into his sad, dark eyes and touched his cheek. I will stay with you tonight.

And so we hunkered down to rest, with his little head in my lap and the enormous draft mare standing above. I paused for a moment to realize that I had met both of these equines just hours earlier. One angry response from this draft and I could be seriously injured, and baby mortally harmed. It seemed ridiculous in the moment of love and compassion, and so we three kept the vigil all night.

Day by day, week upon week, little P and his surrogate mom, Nevada, made progress. Their new life at our little rescue agreed with them and soon they began to look like well-loved horses. Wormed and fed, P was beginning to shine. His eyes began to twinkle and I smiled when bits of his personality would come through. Nevada, our aptly named grand dam, remained sweet, serene and completely comfortable in her role watching over us.

I wasn't sure P could ever be a riding horse because his legs had been so compromised so early on. Nevada, I discovered from researching her brand, was a bucking horse. (Your ride on her was guaranteed to last less than 7 seconds.) So my little rescue contemplated the pair's future when a woman appeared. She had one rescued rodeo horse and was looking for another. Her big, sweet, un-ridable draft mares became her "Retired Rodeo Queens." The Sierra Nevada mountain range is a perfect climate for her girls and updates share they are doing extremely well.

Little P stayed on much longer at the rescue. He made everyone's day with his endless curiosity and happy attitude. If you were in a bad mood, it didn't last long in P's company. One reason is because he had the whitest square teeth I have ever seen on a colt, and thus earned him the nickname "Chicklits."

"Hey Chicklits!" the kids would call.

Romping and shaking his head from side to side was how he'd greet them right back. Head hung over the fence, and soaking up the pets and treats, easily became his most favorite thing to do. And to be certain, make no mistake, when his company left he would stand pouting as if to inquire, "Hey, where could you possibly need to go? I am here! What else is there?"

Sulking away, he would go stand looking out over the pastures rolling away in front of him. P was most definitely a people horse. People made his day, his world. I wondered if it was because of the night the three of us had spent together upon his arrival. He seemed so completely comfortable lying there using me for warmth. It was plain obvious, P just preferred people over his own kind.

And so, we are back to our journey. When we delivered Sunny to Laurie it was another perfect excuse for me to see P. Laurie and P had been keeping company about two years now. Every time I lay eyes on this magnificent Thoroughbred, I am completely taken aback. His beauty, presence, and sheer size are inspiring. His dark bay coat is a dappled reflection of light. His eyes are still coal black. He sports a generous mane and tail, defining that Thoroughbred elegance. He has been transformed from a lost soul clinging to a chance to live to a most exquisite animal. I am moved by his beauty and poise. I promise you, one cannot watch him gallop across a pasture without tears welling up in the eyes. Patriot is poetry. Period.

So with Sunny's arrival at Blue Horse Rescue, the reunion was complete. Little Sunny and Sapphire enjoyed their stay at Blue Horse Rescue. Lots of sunshine and easy, natural training was a daily ritual. Laurie uses trust-based trainers and they do lovely work.

It was a very sad day when the news was brought to me about Sapphire's accident. Many months after Sunny had arrived, little Sapphire was working in a pen and the unthinkable happened. She reared and fell. And then it was over. That fast. A blink of an eye— and she was gone. A freak accident had just occurred. The shock and sadness of losing her was overwhelming. Laurie shared how numbing it is to experience such a loss. The grief and sadness, the confusion, and unanswered questions linger. Why, why...?

Laurie takes comfort from her experience with the energy of Sapphire's mother. The image of a mare, made up of wind and a quiet presence, stood in the distance just on the other side of the fence. She appeared and would reappear, as if to communicate to Laurie and provide her with understanding. Her spirit waited and had called her foal home. I am reassured once again of the connectivity we all share. Mothers and daughters, past lives and present—these relationships each resonate with connection, love, peace, and putting the difficult into perspective. Some people call it faith while others name it destiny or actions of the universe. I believe in my heart it is Spirit. Spirit is God, Love, and the Energy that unites us on both sides of this physical realm. It is Spirit that gives me the strength to takes steps every day on my journey, and thus is held very close to my heart.

I also credit my beliefs for bringing those in need into my world. They cross my path lightly as if to inquire, "Can you help me?" I never feel bombarded or taken advantage of in these times. Each circumstance feels fragile and appreciative. When a situation feels tense, pushed, feigned, or somehow false I know to pause. It is in the moments of taking time that the truth of any situation unfolds and reveals everything needed. To understand how to help a horse, or to be able to control a difficult overbearing personality, I find quiet reflection will provide me the knowledge I need.

I used to be amazed at how pushy and demanding people could behave. Standing as a guest at my facility and acting without any concern for noise, manners, parking, their trash, or even their own dogs. I'm not amazed anymore. I just go into action, dismantling each situation as it occurs. I keep thinking to myself that there is a reason for their visit and it will reveal itself. Be patient. Although, remember the Babbling Mucker? I chalk that up to me understanding myself a little more clearly!

CHAPTER 21

Carius

Late summer of 2012 brought in a request for one of my mares and her filly to keep company with another mare and her filly. The invitation came from a very luxurious dressage barn. The invitation included verdant pastures surrounded by towering redwoods. What a lovely scenario. Foals love the company of other foals and I thought was it would be a nice win-win situation for all involved.

While waiting for the barn owner to come and greet us, I found myself walking through the long aisle of the enormous barn. The ceilings were high; the lighting was way above the stall tops, throwing these linear shadows all over the ground. I had a feeling of complete loneliness. The general aisle was clean and tidy. A small light came from the groomer's corner. I peeked around the wall to find it was empty save for the box of grooming tools on the matted floor. The clock ticked. *What an odd place, I thought.* There wasn't a soul in sight. Were there horses in this building?

There were metal bars across the entire front of each stall and more bars on the front of each stall door. *How did horses hang their* heads out to socialize? How could they greet one another and exchange the daily gossip? And where were they? It was so quiet!

The bars were painted green and the doors were brown. Every thing around me was the same two shades of dark brown and dark green. I glanced at the dirt, the tall surrounding redwood trees, the grounds, and the barn. I had entered a two-dimensional world—one of light and shadow, brown and green—and it felt eerie.

I walked slowly down the center aisle. I saw a pair of eyes look my way and then glance downward. I approached the box and looked through the metal bars. Again, the eyes looked up. There was no response. The shadows placed heavy dark lines across a face, a mane, and a neck.

"Hey," I whispered, "you in there?"

I could see the shadows move as the weight shifted from one hind leg to the other. His head remained low. I repeated myself.

I noticed a small cell-like door with a latch and loophole. I reached up and unlatched the door. It couldn't have been more than a 2-by-2-foot opening. It looked like one of those openings to slip food through when feeding prisoners. Ah, yes, that was it. This was a fancy high-end prison. I wondered to myself, how many prisoners are in this building?

I reached my arm through the feeding window into the stall and hung it down the other side of the wall. I repeated myself in a low quiet tone.

"Hey buddy, you want a scratch?"

Then I heard a soft nicker, ever so low as though trouble may happen should he speak up. He lifted his muzzle very slowly and sniffed my hand.

From my point of view, all I could see was the top of his poll, the area between his ears, and a luxurious thick patch of mane. I stretched to try and see along the inside wall. His muscles rippled against a massive frame. This horse was huge.

His breath was warm on my hand and I turned palm up lightly to touch his muzzle. He moved in closer. I scratched under his chin. He lifted his head and looked directly into my eyes.

"Get me out."

I furrowed my brow. My hand stroked the underside of his jaw. Then I slid my palm over the bridge of his nose.

This magnificent animal asked again, "Can you get me out?"

I stood there looking into his one, unblinking, demanding eye.

The world can speak to us in many ways. It comes when we least expect it, and sometimes when we really don't want it. This was one of those moments I didn't want it. After all, what could I do for this horse? This gorgeous, unbelievably trained, expensive athlete was asking to be free. I stood there with my hand on his neck. He moved a step forward and my hand slid onto his shoulder. I shouldn't even be touching him, let alone setting him free! He shifted his weight and lifted his head above the stall threshold. With a curve of his neck and a turn of his massive head toward me, he had us looking into one another's eyes.

"I'll do whatever I can," I mumbled. *What the hell was happening to me?*

What can I do? The information came fast and furious. I was getting all kinds of "knowing." I was feeling overwhelmed. I pulled my hand back out of the opening.

I stepped back and took in the sight before me. He looked directly into my eyes. He didn't flinch.

I reached over and pulled the stall door open just slightly. Heaven help me. My movements were not my own. My thoughts weren't functioning. I slipped inside. He was enormous, towering above me. I took in the smell of shavings and urine. He moved into me and placed his head directly into my chest. I held his neck on either side.

"I am so sorry."

My voice was barely a whisper. My thoughts continued to race.

I must be here to help. I believe I would not have been sent to witness your suffering if there was not a way for me to help. I am breaking the law right now. Shit. I will try my best not to let you down. I will try my best for you.

The sound of a truck wheels in the dirt had me springing to the outside of the stall.

"I promise, I will be back."

Door closed, latch checked. I briskly walked to the entrance to meet the woman who owns the facility.

The cutest little elf of a woman slid down out of a building-sized truck. She had fiery, curly, red hair and soft green eyes that smiled and danced as she spoke.

"Hi! Welcome. I am Gennie, come meet baby!"

Her excitement and pride would not be contained as her 5-foot frame trotted across the landscape to the first stall in an adjacent barn. I stood back as she pulled the stall door to one side. I was chuckling at the picture of her. *Piece of work,* I thought, observing her cowboy boots and jean capris that sat barely past the knee-caps, leaving her bare ivory-colored legs exposed. Teeny tiny arms reached up and stroked the massive neck of mama horse. On went the halter and out she came.

Spitfire, hell-on-wheels was not far behind. She bolted out of the stall and then paused to take in her surroundings. I stopped to catch my breath. There are no words created to define the beauty that stood before me. Every inch of this foal at 4 months old was perfect. Her dark eyes surveyed the scene. Her head was poised and confident. Wow. I was speechless. *So this is what imported European warmblood foals look like.*

"Come, baby come!" Gennie was motioning for the filly to follow mom.

Off she went! Where was the starting gate? She bolted and broke into a canter across the yard. *Flying lead changes at 4 months old, really?* I didn't know it was possible. Tail straight in the air, she settled into a floating trot. *Were her hooves touching the ground?* It was tough to tell. The filly, realizing she had put a substantial piece of real estate between herself and mama, let out a whinny and broke into a full gallop back across the yard. Into the pasture she bolted. Gennie and momma were her target. Gennie threw her arms around her neck and the baby stood heaving breaths of air.

"Wow."

"Isn't she something?" Gennie smiled and continued. "We are so happy you are here. Baby needs company."

I immediately liked this woman. Her quirky style, her crazy hair, and contagious enthusiasm had me sold. She clearly adored horses.

I learned that her Hanoverian filly's mother had died. This lovely mama was a nurse mare. I explained that Margo, the mare I had hauled in, was not Genevieve's mother either. Gennie described all kinds of technicalities to me about papers, birth certificates, and lineage. This filly was already a superstar having earned a prestigious prize of some sort for being the best looking filly in her class for the year.

What I most enjoyed was the lack of concern amongst these equines about who really belonged to whom. Paper and lineage, even mothers, didn't really matter. They were safe. They had a gorgeous home and lots of room to romp. The protective "mothers" cantered alongside the little ones while they frolicked and played.

It felt a little odd. I pondered what I had just experienced a moment before. When do they go to prison? How long do they get to be horses before they go in cages here?

We said our goodbyes, promised to check in, and I silently made a solemn vow to go back and see that horse.

CHAPTER 22

Bear Makes His Debut

Once Margo and Genevieve had been safely delivered, I felt a glass of wine was in order. I've decided it must be a way for me to mitigate stress. The stress of knowing the need for help is so great, and the effort for each save is so tremendous. However, I learned a very valuable lesson about the dangers of chardonnay and Facebook. While sipping, please note it's best to lock your "I-Can-Save-The-World" button into the off position! Of course I'm speaking of my irrational need to find dogs!

I found myself falling in love with an old soul in Orange County. His pitiful mug was filled with disbelief at where he had landed. It's bad enough to be beaten up when you're a senior, but then to be abandoned? Unbelievable. Dumped at the shelter by his owners who were not interested in paying a vet bill, he arrived with scratch and bite marks on both front legs. His chances of being adopted were slim to none. I committed to this boy and found myself a couple of days later on a quick jaunt to meet the folks transporting him. At first they were going to bring him to me but that's a heck of a drive—some 700 miles—so I offered to meet them halfway.

Coalinga, California, is a lovely town of 16,000. Never saw one citizen as I was trying my darnedest to get back to the interstate. How did I end up here...? I was trying to be clever without GPS.

My girlfriend Katy asked by text message, "How's your new pup?"

"Old, like me," I replied. "Also, I'm a bit lost."

Oh boy, she's worse than me when it come to directions. I could just feel her panic in that moment.

"No worries," I quickly dashed off. "Onward and northward!"

What's not to love? He was a great little traveler chewing on his water cup, lifting it above his head, the last drop landing in his eye. We visited and shared our life stories. He was looking forward to meeting the big dogs. I told him to keep an eye on the feet, and he'd be just fine. Not a peep, not a whimper. He sat looking out the window the entire ride. Every now and then he'd glance my way. His little blink was a check in as if to say, "OK, this will work!"

I ran out of gas due to getting lost in Coalinga. I parked at the gas station and in 60 minutes I was back on the road. My son has bailed me out of many a quandary. I am eternally grateful for his help, his smile, and a "no problem" attitude. I pulled into the ranch at around 9:30 that night. My quick little jaunt had lasted nine hours. It's true. One can survive on Doritos and water.

Once home, Bear sauntered around checking out his new digs. The other dogs were waggin' around, smiling, and welcoming the senior citizen into the pack.

I will share that we hold many lovely spiritual workshops and classes at the rescue, and the next morning we were scheduled to host about eight guests. "Walking the Prayer Wheel" is a spiritual practice honoring the sacredness of life. Clients learn all about what the structure of the wheel symbolizes. I particularly like the notion that the "center is the beginning of life, the place where birth, the young and life's beginnings reside." At one of our previously held Saturday classes, Native American visitors had brought blessed stones from sacred burial grounds.

As that day's workshop progressed, we observed that all the horses out in pasture had mimicked our posture and the babies were in the center of the sacred circle, sleeping. I also noticed Bear had inserted himself into the circle. He was participating as though it was expected of him. When the people stood, so did Bear. And when they sat, he joined them. I couldn't help but think that this little, old, beat-up pit bull was giving thanks for his second chance at life. He was honoring the powers that be. He made his rounds quietly, accepting pats on the head whenever possible. All the mares stood looking on quietly. They had created their own sacred wheel to honor life. We were feeling very blessed and connected. These experiences are truly a gift.

So imagine my horror when tidying up the following day when I noticed my rocks were gone! I looked around to see where in the heck these mini boulders had disappeared. Who might have moved them? The trailer was close by, and so I stooped to peek underneath. *Nope, no rocks.* I was confused.

It was then I noticed a couple of our dogs hanging out, layin' around like dogs do. "Did you guys take my rocks?"

Deoge, Robert's pup, looked at me like "what are you talking about?" He turned away and casually looked the other way. Bear was doing that blinky thing with his eyes, which translates to, "Nope, not me...don't look at me. Whatever it is, I didn't do it." Then up he went and headed to the garage. Jake stood watching him leave. I think I heard him mumble under his bad doggy breath, "You're a big liar."

Beardog must have been feeling the love. Tracking him to his little nest in the garage revealed the rocks. Tucked in and "buried" under his favorite blankie.

Well, well, what have we here? I was chuckling to myself. I picked up the rocks and tucked them away. I gave Bear a new toy and went inside. A few minutes later I opened the door and there he stood, looking at me.

I swear he was saying, "Where are my rocks?"

CHAPTER 23

Under Attack!

It was a shock. We were all completely blindsided. The attack came unannounced. No eyes witnessed the actual attack, but we are all certain it was over food. Anna-Moose was screaming and I spun around to find her being shaken like a rag doll! I grabbed the tail of the culprit and began to pull back. Jillian and the husband jumped into the middle, pulling dogs apart. Released from the jaws of death, I reached down to scoop up Anna-Moose.

"Ouch! Augh!" She bit me. I clutched her to my chest and ran into the house. I lay her down on the floor in the bathroom and reached up to get a towel. I saw her shaking and lying there. Blood began to pool under her.

Oh my God. Hang on, I thought. Just hang on.

It was a long night at the emergency hospital. We were expecting the worst. Three hours passed and the vet appeared.

"She is in the oxygen tank," she began slowly. "It appears she has multiple puncture wounds. Her skin under her left forearm has been ripped and she may have a hernia. We'd like to see if there is any internal damage. Her organs may be compromised."

I looked at Jillian, and she at me. Is there any worse feeling in the world than having to consider if there is enough money to keep those you love alive? In an instant, the worst dog in the world was relying on me and I felt like a pitiful failure. We discussed all our options with this lovely vet. Surgery was not one of them. We didn't have upwards of $6,000. Hell, I don't even have enough money to meet all my monthly bills. She was kind, reassuring and non-judgmental. I appreciated her so very much.

"Let's keep her overnight. We can watch her, give intravenous antibiotics, and pain medication. We will know better in the morning if she has a chance."

Jillian and I went in and blew her a kiss goodbye. We talked all the way home about how much we had taken our little Moose for granted. We laughed at how she could jump four times her height in order to get your attention.

Jillian mused, "Remember we almost named her Sister Bertrille?"

Her ears are so large that we giggled at the thought of naming her after the infamous Flying Nun. We remembered that even though she was loud and never ever listened to anyone, she loved us so wholeheartedly. She lived for us every day. We were her world. She deserved the chance to live, and so Jillian and I made a promise that if she rallied overnight we'd find a way to keep her alive.

Morning came and she had stabilized! She was out of the oxygen tank, breathing on her own. Her gums were pink and she even wagged her little tail. The vet thought these were very positive signs. It was recommended she stay another night. The vet then offered her monthly stipend of $200 to cover the anesthesia so that X-rays could be taken. My heart was so full. Her generosity was enormously gracious.

Two broken ribs, multiple puncture wounds, sutures, a hernia, and an Elizabethan collar all came home with Anna-Moose. Her pain medication was working. She wagged her little tail until her loopy eyes rolled back into her head and she fell asleep. She was secure. She confidently and happily placed her very life in my arms.

"She completely believes in us mom."

"Yeah, I know."

"We won't let her down. We will make sure she gets better."

I needed her optimism. I looked at my daughter and silently thanked her for every thing she was, everything she shared, and her eternal opinion that love is always the better path.

Recovery wasn't fast enough for the Moose. Keeping her quiet and rested was not her idea of rehabilitation. Getting out of her crate as often as possible to harass Jake was a much better plan in her mind. And so the days passed and Anna-Moose healed up. Her attitude didn't change one single bit. She still thinks she's boss. She is still in charge. Her complete recovery is a daily reminder to share love every day.

It is a gift. It remains true. Sharing love is the biggest gift anyone can give. It comes in the form of warmth, security, forgiveness, and understanding. The list is long. My mom used to tell me that "water seeks its own level." Like-minded, generous, loving, committed people come into my world. Their generosity and care fills my heart as I watch them make commitments to love and care for these animals for a lifetime. We come from many different backgrounds and experiences. We all share the same vision of kindness and love. We walk the prayer wheel and send healing energy from afar. We gentle and train the babies for their jobs in life. We find new homes for the senior citizens. It's a good feeling to help.

CHAPTER 24

Understanding Reiki

t was a Saturday morning and to call it glorious does not do the day justice. The blue sky was piercing in early November and the temperature was perfect. I picked up my rake and began spreading the sand in my new round pen. I had a group of Reiki healers working on the horses. Reiki is a form of alternative medicine developed in 1922 by Japanese Buddhist Mikao Usui. It is a Japanese technique for stress reduction and relaxation, and it also promotes healing. It is administered by "laying on hands" and is based on the idea that an unseen "life force energy" flows through us, causing us to be alive.

When the healers are present, the area becomes very peaceful. The horses all find a person to approach and begin their journey to bliss. Eyes flutter and their heads begin to lower in relaxation. It's one of the things I absolutely love about observing Reiki on horses. The horses physically manifest the energy work. If you have doubts about the healing effects of energy work, go watch it done on horses. They hold no barriers. They are connected to their own energy 100 percent of the time. They begin to lick and chew (a sure sign of contentment), and the babies often lie down to sleep and rest.

I was raking the mounds of sand, enjoying the pattern it created. It reminded me of the satisfaction I get from vacuuming. I love to see the pattern on the rugs. This sand was top quality, a little bit damp, and was holding every imprinted stoke. The rake began to make a soft humming sound. I felt a knowing that I was being told to hold the handle lightly. *Let your palms direct the push and pull, no need to grasp it so tight. Try to let the rake flow over the sand.* It was within these moments I felt the rhythm and motion begin to carry me into an easy peace. Shadows moving from the towering eucalyptus kept the breeze brisk and cleansing.

My dear teacher and Reiki Master, Leah, popped over and suggested, "Lynn, come get some Reiki."

Sitting in a chair, I closed my eyes and began to think about relaxing. I took a breath and began to let the tightness down. First my chest, then my thighs slowly began to quiet. I felt hands lay softly upon my knees, another pair of hands upon my shoulders.

Ah, the feel of touch, so nice. It was so welcome to this weary body. I began to focus on the dark as I looked at the inside of my eyelids. I saw a few pieces of light flicker and disappear. I was concentrating on quiet. I began to see clouds. A sepia tone fog began to roll in from the periphery. And then there was a face. I concentrated on the face and it became bigger. It looked Native American. It was expressionless. Closer and larger, clearer, it remained motionless. As it floated to the right, another image appeared on the left. It was another face, another Native American face. I looked into his eyes of this man. He was calm, peaceful. I felt I was being told to continue, and to not give up. I was assured that I was not struggling alone. I almost would define the moment as being gently scolded.

It was as if the image, the man, was stating, "You think your struggle is large. STOP. Be guided by the heart. Always follow the heart." And then three more images all came to me, all expressing the same thought. "We are here. We acknowledge and honor your work".

As the practical mind will do, I began to worry that I was making this up. Some horse was wearing a blanket and it needed removing. Waters needed to be checked. My untrained mind began to wander—looking for the practical, the doable. With perfect timing, the hands on my shoulders shifted ever so slightly and snapped me back. STOP. I refocused my efforts.

She appeared quietly and within gray, slim cloud cover. Her face was partially veiled, a scarf flowing and dancing in the winds until it became a cloud thinning out and floating away from my view. My first thought was that this must be the Virgin Mother, the Virgin Mary. All of my childhood lessons of Jesus and his mother circled my thoughts. But on closer inspection I saw she too was Native American. To speak without words, sending messages of love and hope, is a powerful moment. She looked into my eyes, her scarf once again changing shape. She was the mother who nurtured and cared for the young—a gentle hand touching a cheek and a comfort to the newly born. This is Mother Love. I was engulfed with a sense of warmth and comfort. I felt like the child on the couch watching cartoons while dinner fragrances waft from the kitchen. I felt safe, loved and so utterly content.

The Reiki session came to a soft and comfortable close. We all sat for a moment in the quiet. As I began to share my experience with the group, it was explained to me that many Native American rituals began with the raking of the land. It is the combing of Mother Earth's hair.

The "Language and Sacredness of Hair is taught by All Tribal People of Earth," writes Paula Johnstone-Whitehawk in her article "Hair Raising...A Spiritual Journey."

She continues, "The way a People comb (the alignment of thought), braid (the oneness of thought), tie (the securing of thought), and color (the conviction in thought) their hair is of great significance."

I reflected on all the times I had participated in this ritual with my mother, and then again with my own little girl. These timeless rituals have been performed perhaps for centuries. I smiled and thought to myself that comfort and love is truly timeless.

CHAPTER 25

Margo, Genevieve

Autumn had arrived and that meant it was time for Margo, the surrogate mother, to wean Genevieve up at the fancy dressage barn. Baby Genevieve would stay to keep the warmblood filly company and perhaps find her adoptive home there. That was the initial plan anyway.

Upon our arrival, I found my mare and her filly out in a grand pasture. Alongside them was the stunning filly. Where was the mom? A short conversation revealed that mom had passed away. Died. The language used gave the impression the mare was elderly. The age of 22 is not elderly in my world. Horses can, do, and should live well into their early 30s, some even into their 40s. And I have met a 50-year-old equine, and so my thoughts were troubled.

I understand very well that it's not just our culture, but also our world that puts tremendous pressure on young horses. They race and perform and execute extraordinary tasks well before they are physically matured to do so. This results in broken down legs, tendons, and bodies that are "old" well before their time. The heart-break for me is that this has become the norm. Another present-day attitude is that a horse in its teenage years is well past its prime. It is expected to be close to, if not already, relying upon supplements and painkillers to be "useful." Of course this breaks my heart, infuriates my good sense, and makes me personally want to scream, "When does the abuse stop?"

I was annoyed at this latest news and looking for an excuse to bring both my horses home, then I realized I didn't need one. Her filly was wearing a halter and used to being handled. My mare and little filly were regressing. They were wary and uncomfortable about being approached. Hmm. My brain began to churn. *What has transpired here?* Something negatively affecting my mare and this filly has occurred. I would find out soon enough.

Meantime, I was in a hurry to get down the barn aisle to find the big dark horse. Looking around, I didn't see any bodies moving about. These big barns are kind of eerie. And, just as before, the place was like a morgue. I figured I had a few minutes before Gennie arrived. I am big on keeping my promises and was looking forward to seeing this big boy. I approached his stall with anticipation and then my stomach sank.

It was empty. Fresh shavings and an empty stall were all that remained. There was no trace of him. No nametag on the door and no vet instructions in the transparent index cardholder still tacked to the wall. He was gone. *Oh my God.* How could I ever locate this horse? I was disappointed with myself for not making a larger effort. I waited too long to get back up there. I should have taken the time. I scolded myself for my transgression. I felt sad that I was not able to help. I wanted to complete a promise. Not knowing where he was or his circumstance was just awful. I felt empty inside. I had let him down. I pondered all the different places he could end up. He was so unhappy. Now I was unhappy too. This horrible knot welled up inside of me.

"Are you looking for Carius?" a woman's voice inquired.

I didn't know his name. I was caught a bit off guard and unsettled by her question, having presumed I was alone.

"Um yes, I just wanted to say hello."

"I'm sorry. You just missed him. He left this morning, about 8."

Carius. I had his name.

I blurted out, "Do you know where he went? I mean did he move for good?"

The woman smiled and replied, "Yes, he's left for good, but I don't know where."

Now my spirits were really down. How could I have failed him?

"Thank you," was all I could say. I glanced up to find she was already walking away and out of earshot. I smiled a small, weary smile and walked toward the exit, heading to the pasture where Gen and Margo awaited. They were both coming home.

An email was waiting for me at home explaining that Gennie had tried to wean my filly from her momma mare. Without many details I am presuming it didn't go too well. She was annoyed with me because I had left her filly in the pasture alone. Her filly was fine with many horses in sight. Never mind that she took liberties with my mare and foal without permission, and certainly without the skill needed! The look of fear and anticipation on their faces had said it all. I glanced out my window and was relieved to see both mom and filly in my pasture, back at the rescue where they belonged and were understood.

This experience is again one of the daily problems with horse people. Some trainers and barn managers are so capable, so gentle and qualified. The others are impatient, constantly creating their own agendas for the horses (which never works), and ultimately doing emotional damage. How on earth can one know? How can one assess the talent of an individual without standing and observing? My answer is that I don't think you can. It's such a difficult task. The horses rely upon us to make sure they are placed with the aforementioned horse person and not the latter.

The term or title "Natural Horsemanship" is very popular now. It's used as an effort to define the quiet, talented, preferred horse person. The methodology of training focuses on building trust and creating a partnership. '"Horse-Whisperer" is another term that is often heard or read about and this title carries even more mystery and talent with it. The title suggests the horse person can read the subtle cues, interpret, and communicate so effectively with the horse that it becomes a language unto itself. To witness this kind of relationship leaves me in awe and inspired. There is an even newer term utilized as people continue to search for that elusive label to really explain the magic that can occur. "Relationship Training" stresses the importance of creating trust and a bond before beginning the task of teaching.

Within these circles of professionals it is not acceptable to tire a horse out by lunging them in circles. It is unproductive to send a horse round and round while smacking a whip to the dirt. It is actually counterproductive, as the horse remains confused and somewhat nervous or frightened when he or she simply carries out this learned helplessness to stay out of trouble. One must remember, for every moment you're using these old techniques, the further you and your horse move away from what's possible. If a horse has pent up energy why not turn them out? Let them have options to buck, kick, gallop, fart (always!), and choose to shake their heads. Once settled with some of that energy spent, the lunging without a lead line can begin to teach a horse the exercise and game of bending, collecting, etc. The Carolyn Resnick method is a wonderful example of this groundwork-focused partnership. I reason that if one individual can accomplish this then don't all horses deserve it? I tucked my latest question into my pocket and thought I would ponder this further later. Right now I was thinking about Carius.

I grabbed my laptop and Googled the name Carius. Just what kind of name was Carius? I had a name and no location. How does one track down a horse without any more information than that? Just how many barns are there in the nation, not to mention private facilities? I felt saddened and hopeless.

The definition revealed that Carius was the son of Zeus. Hmm. *He's big enough to be the son of Zeus.* Carius, as the legend is written, is believed to have learned music from the nymphs. Well, I didn't think this was much help as I thought of Carius and wondered where his life had taken him. I hoped he indeed was playing music in his heart and not suffering. I held a lingering sadness, feeling as though I had let him down.

Months passed and my lingering sadness stayed with me. Pushing it away from my thoughts provided a moment's distraction. I kept telling myself there was absolutely nothing I could do. I became very comfortable talking to Spirit, asking for the safety and happiness of my giant friend. I was also selfishly asking for a sign.

CHAPTER 26

Jillian, Jove And Whiskey

By 2012, my daughter Jillian was nearly 18 years old. As her beloved boy Whiskey came closer to retiring from being a riding horse, she fell in love with a second horse for riding. Whiskey remained working, filling an important role in my childrens' programs. These non-riding workshops give all children the chance to encounter and experience horses. Here they get to touch them, learn about them, watch their ears, and find out more about how they think and live. Whiskey has an enormous place of honor as the gelding on the property and the ambassador of The Pregnant Mare Rescue. Why a gelding, you ask? Well, it's not because he is a gelding, as a mare could fill the role nicely. It is because of his trustworthiness. He is so well behaved with people so he is trusted with the most shy and conservative of visitors. He stands while visitors touch and pat him. They stroke his neck and lift his feet. He never moves. He keeps everybody safe. He allows complete strangers to fumble around his face while learning how to put on a halter. They lead and he follows. They stop and he stops. He graciously turns on his magic every time a class is held. At 31 years young, he is the picture of health and a valuable asset to the program.

What I find enormously humorous and annoying at the very same time is what a fat jerk he is with all the mares. He is so mean and bossy that he is usually pastured next to them instead of with them. Everyone, however, loves Whiskey. He is sassy, confident, charming, and very handsome.

Jillian's second love hails from the Netherlands. Napoleon, or Leo for short, is a huge Dutch warmblood. I was told that in 2006 he was on the Olympic team representing the Netherlands. This would be quite impressive! He was now in his early 20s and found himself working in a jumping barn when the email came across my desk. Can you guess? He had sustained an injury that would require a lengthy rehabilitation; the barn was interested in rehoming him. Are you kidding me? Leo was on his way to California.

He may have been one of the largest horses I have ever laid eyes on. He was big and powerful, but his face was like that of a little puppy with the kindest, sweetest eyes and curiosity a mile long. Welcome, Leo! Welcome to your new forever home. Jillian was giddy. I made sure Whiskey didn't pout.

Jillian, Leo and Jillian's phone spent countless hours together. All three were inseparable. I decided it was time for me to have a companion of my own.

I was browsing the Internet, looking at rescues run by friends, and looking for a horse needing a home. I came across a lovely Thoroughbred in his mid teens. Jove was his name. Jove is derived from the word Jupiter and Jupiter is the God of Abundance. Well, I liked that. Abundance is good!

Jove was living at a prestigious university up in Palo Alto, California, which isn't too far from us. I made an appointment to visit. Jillian and I arrived on a gorgeous sunny morning. As many people are well aware, this school has a very impressive campus. The horse facilities are impeccable. Huge bronze statues of stunning equines graced the fine trimmed lawns. Every corral clean, every horse beautiful, and everything in perfect order. But I wasn't fooled. The last prestigious barn I visited had broken my heart. I would proceed with caution.

We entered and began to take in what lay before us. Everything was painted white. Wash racks, tie areas, restrooms, and washing machines. I felt as though I was in a hospital ward and for good reason. I had walked into the area designated for medical visits and laundry. Oops. Rounding a corner, I found what looked much more like a barn. We were greeted by rows of horses hanging their lovely heads into the center aisle. Chatting and visiting, they were curious as to who we were.

"New visitors! Yay, check for treats!"

They stretched their necks as far into the center of the aisle as was physically possible. I had to chuckle. We found the office and we introduced ourselves to the barn manager, Vanessa. She was friendly and warm. She suggested we take a walk to go see Jove. He was already standing in the crossties.

"Well, hello, Jove."

He stood obediently and looked into my eyes. *Beautiful boy,* I thought. Vanessa saddled him up and began chatting about all things Jove. His likes, dislikes, habits, and diet.

I inquired, "Why is he being rehomed?"

"He doesn't like his job."

I thought I had heard incorrectly. When did it matter to humans whether or not a horse liked his job?

"Really?" I had to pause.

She looked up from his side and smiled.

"We want our horses to be happy here. We think they deserve to be healthy and happy. Dressage just isn't his thing."

Jillian shot me a look of utter shock.

I raised my eyebrows and replied, "Wow, how refreshing to hear."

Saddled up and ready to go, we walked out to an enormous covered arena. Jillian would be the first to mount. I was intimidated as riding is NOT my forte. She began with a slow walk in each direction and then proceeded to take up the trot.

He moved so smooth, so beautiful. His coat was the color of dark eggplant. He was so shiny he looked fresh out of the shower. I stood listening to the rhythm of his breathing. Jill closed her fingers and his head rounded, tucking closer to his chest. *Whoa, this horse is amazing.*

I looked to Vanessa and commented, "He will be teaching me."

She laughed and said he would make an excellent instructor. It was my turn to hop on, and I was feeling very inadequate. I took Jove's reins and announced we were going to take a small walk, a moment if you will, just to say hello. We strolled the grounds and I chatted away about what daily life would be like back on the ranch. He looked at me with a great curiosity. I'm certain he was thinking that nobody has ever done this. *What are you doing walking with me?* I kept smiling and chatting.

Finally Jill said, in her kindest coaching voice, "Get over it mom, you're fine."

I smiled and up I went.

"He's a tall boy," I winced. And so we began.

With all the care taken like that of a bodyguard, he carried me around the arena. I was talking to him, telling him how amazing I found him to be. I was telling him that his days trotting around in circles like this would be over. I envisioned long lazy trails with shaded picnic stops. I apologized for not spending a few days before hopping on his back. I hoped he got the message. He felt happy to me and so pleased for the compliment. His appreciation made him glow. Up to the trot we progressed, and I felt I was floating upon the sea. Up and down, a steady rhythm, rocking forward and back. Posting the trot felt easy, so effortless!

Oh, I like this boy! I dismounted and hugged him. I stroked his neck and looked into his eye. Ok. I thought. *We are partners. Deal?* He nudged my shoulder and Jillian and I laughed at his timing. As we all strolled back toward the barn, I was learning all I could about my new boy.

Once back inside, I noticed it was full of activity. There was a class going on over in the crossties. A horse stood dutifully while questions that sounded veterinarian-ish were answered. In another corner, a couple of cute girls were fussing over their horses, chatting it up. I liked the energy and the hum of folks hanging out, grooming, and talking horses. It felt so nice. I had been completely wrong in my presumption. This barn was superb. I liked everything about it.

There was a nicker from my left side and I turned expecting to see yet another horse being led in the aisle way, or stretching for treats. There was a man who was obviously teaching a class, his hand resting on this gelding in the crossties. He had stopped his lecture to inquire about Jove.

"How was he?" he asked.

"Fabulous!" I smiled.

"Really a nice boy!" I could not contain my grin.

"Isn't he? So glad you like him. We all love him!"

It was in that instant I glanced at the gelding standing quietly. I looked at his eyes and he threw his head up. He nickered and lifted a front hoof. He pawed at the matt underneath.

"Carius?" I inquired.

The man's face lit up as he asked, "You know Carius?"

I was stunned. I was at a loss for words. I had a group of eight people looking at me and waiting for my reply. I could see their thoughts spinning. Do you or don't you?

"Um, kind of, well, yes, but not very well." I slopped my way through an answer. I moved forward toward him and the class stepped aside. I felt like I was parting the sea!

"Well, he certainty knows you."

Once again his massive head tucked into my chest. I felt my tears well up, a knot sitting in my throat. This time I heard, "I am loved. I am good."

I stroked his neck and explained to my audience that we had met briefly at his old barn. I had just been a bit concerned about how happy he was living there.

"Really, we were just acquaintances." I explained.

The instructor began sharing just what a fabulous horse Carius is and all the wonderful things he teaches the students. I was smitten with the idea of this magnificent animal having his own fan club. No more lonely hours in a quiet empty barn. Solitary confinement was over. The giggling girls told tales of warm baths and spa days full of grooming and fussing. A chunky little cherub stepped forward, her face full of freckles.

"I just adore him!" she pronounced.

Her arms supported her excitement as she lifted them high above her head. She was gesturing to me and hugging him at the same time.

"I come see him every chance I get!"

Her enthusiasm left me warm and content. *Well, OK, Carius, I* thought, *life is very good.* I quietly reflected and thanked Spirit for the good news—and for sharing it with me. I now put all the puzzle pieces together. The trip to the fancy dressage barn wasn't at all about Margo and Genevieve or the stunning filly. It was for Carius and a lesson for me to learn about making generalizations. It was a lesson for me to understand that each circumstance is its own. Do not generalize. Lynn, look at both big fancy barns and appreciate the difference in attitude and the treatment of the horses. I have noted that even the difference of the V-space for the horses to hang their heads out of their paddocks can be life changing for them. They need to connect!

Jillian and I entered Vanessa's office to make arrangements to bring my new boy home. I could feel myself smiling.

CHAPTER 27

Let's Make A Change!

As the years have passed, our experiences and lessons have continually grown. Many horses are unwanted or used up, discarded, uncared for, either orphaned or pregnant—all conditions that reflect a sorry state of affairs for our beloved equines. So, where is the change?

I originally wanted to understand why horses are treated so poorly in all countries by almost everyone, leading us to the need for horse "rescue." How did mass ignorance occur when it comes to handling, training, and riding these magnificent creatures? Where is the appreciation?

I have learned that by insulting or condemning any one specific culture, country or continent one cannot make generalizations. I observe an extreme lack of understanding of what equines are capable of physically, spiritually, and emotionally by people all over the world. It simply exists everywhere. I conclude it is the condition of being human. The answer to changing treatment of horses all over the world lies in baby steps. Once again, it's the old adage of each individual taking the first small step. Patience, pausing to think before taking action, or considering partnership over dominance can be the beginning of change.

I mentioned early on my thoughts on the human agenda. Yes, dirty, egotistical, and financial motivation is unfortunately alive and well. But what about good old folks who own horses and believe in their heart of hearts they are doing right by them? My answer is they don't know any different or ego is blinding. They have been taught a certain way to achieve desired results and that's what they do. It's all they know. And changing a mind or habit is a pretty tough thing to do, even if one was instructed on how to do so.

Financial implications play a large part. Horses either cost too much to keep or, sometimes, earning a buck is the only goal. Laziness and convenience also play a part. Then there is ego—and ego plays a big part. Let me restate that. EGO plays the biggest role in keeping horses misunderstood and abused. I've heard it said that if horses could scream then things would be a lot different. Can you let go for your horse, for the love of horse?

Every single circumstance that brings about abuse to a horse is some combination of these four issues coming into play: ego, finances, convenience, and laziness. This is in effect right now, every day, all over the world. There are folks who really get it right 100 percent. They can help us all become better horse people. They can help us all understand how to really be with, train, love, ride, and enjoy horses without any abuse. But, in my honest and humble opinion, I would say that 80 percent of horse folk I encounter get it wrong.

I'll address the financial motivation first. Here are examples of money-making ventures that I believe put horses at high risk for abuse: most racing, some breeding and selling, some riding instruction, all Premarin (estrogen industry) mares, all nurse mares and their discarded foals, and all the wild mustangs being eradicated off our public lands. The arguments for racing, breeding, selling and riding are ever-present, controversial, and an ethical dilemma that goes round and round for me, which is why I preface my statement with "most" or "some." But my stance is unwavering on the subjects of the nurse mares and their foals, Premarin mares, and our wild mustangs.

First let's talk about my experiences with nurse mare foals because the financial implications are demonstrated at their very worst. A nurse mare foal is a baby who was born so that its mother might come into milk. The milk that its mother is producing is used to nourish a more expensive foal of another mare. You see, the expensive foal has an expensive mom, and that mom needs to get back to work. Primarily these are Thoroughbred mares and foals, though this practice is certainly not limited to the Thoroughbred industry. The foal of the mother that came into milk is then discarded. They are literally born to die. They used to be clubbed to death but that became frowned upon—or perhaps too much trouble—and they were simply left to starve. Now rescues hearing of their plight step up to take them, and so conveniently they suddenly have an asking price of $25 to $100. (Of course, I am using sarcasm here to deflect my disgust at what humans are capable of doing.)

One year Pregnant Mare Rescue decided to work with the Last Chance Corral out of Athens, Ohio. This organization specializes in the discarded foals from the Thoroughbred breeding industry. We paid $800 dollars and pulled a number of foals, committing to place them in good homes. We set up what became known as the PMR Orphan Train. Interested parties all along the trail, from Ohio to California, filled out adoption applications. We would be the last stop on the journey west. It took a lot of communication and time, but we eventually had homes approved as the hauler headed our direction. Every home fulfilled their agreement with the exception of two, and those little fillies would be staying with us until we found them homes.

Enya and Sunshine, the little light-colored, fuzzy, chestnut girls with white markings adorning their foreheads, huddled together in their new paddock. Fresh shavings and warm California sun made their new digs comfy and cozy. Sunshine was the picture of easiness and contentment. Enya was a feisty little kicker, spinning her fanny toward any of us at a moment's notice. Ear pinning was her specialty! These foals were probably 4 weeks old and they had just travelled across the country. Already off of bottles, they quite happily slurped formula from their buckets, sharing milky mustaches and dripping whiskers all around.

A nurse mare foal is an interesting situation because they have not been abused or neglected, they have just never had a moment to experience a mother horse. They are placed with other "orphaned foals" moments after birth. This circumstance creates a conundrum for me. Mammals have mothers and those mothers serve a purpose. They provide so much more than mother's milk. These foals are not like snakes or turtles, destined to survive from birth alone. So, we humans step in and provide the basic care and comfort but I remain curious about the missing piece. A "mother" has such an important role.

Our beloved American mustang—being eradicated by the BLM that was to protect them—is another concern. Remember that they are a national treasure? The motivation behind these operations is plain and simple. Money. The BLM has created a falsehood that there are too many horses on the plains. They state that overpopulation is a problem. I don't buy it. Reality is there is no problem and never was. The BLM is in bed with the cattle ranchers and they want to allow them grazing access for free on our public lands. This translates to (you guessed it) money. If you believe that overpopulation is a problem, or that the mustangs are starving and in ill health, I would press you to do more investigating. While mustangs are hardy, scrappy, healthy survivors, life in the wild is considerably shorter than life in domestication. They do not live as long as domesticated horses. They are also stewards of the earth. They eat grasses without pulling out the roots, till the soil with their hooves, and leave fertilizer in the form of fresh manure as they move. Biologically designed to graze 18 hours a day, every day, makes the horse a supporter to an ecosystem. But, just as in any heated political argument, the facts will be skewed and presented as an argument for removing horses rather than cattle.

Please enjoy the truth. The following is a website excerpt about the American mustang from the highly respected experts at American Wild Horse Campaign:

The Wild Free-Roaming Horse and Burro Act recognizes the wild horse as an "integral component of the natural system." It stipulates that horses can only be removed from public lands if it is proven that they are overpopulating or are causing habitat destruction. It further mandates that the government "maintain specific ranges on public lands as sanctuaries for their protection and preservation."

In order to remove wild horses from public lands, the Bureau of Land Management (BLM) has claimed that horses are destroying critical habitat, competing for grazing lands, and overpopulating. But reports by the General Accounting Office and the National Academy of Sciences dispute such claims: BLM has never presented any evidence that horses destroy habitat, nor that their population levels are what it claims they are. In fact, reducing horse populations in a given area has a negligible effect on range conditions: after massive wild horse roundups, herd areas show little or no improvement, especially in instances when cattle numbers remain the same (or increase).

In stark contrast with BLM's assertions, scientific studies have shown that horses actually benefit their environment in numerous ways; vegetation seems to thrive in some areas inhabited by horses, which may be one reason the Great Plains were once a "sea of grass." Generally, range conditions in steep hilly areas favored by horses are much better than in lower areas frequented by cattle.

Cows have no upper front teeth, only a thick pad: they graze by wrapping their long tongues around grass and pulling on it. If the ground is wet, they will pull out the grass by the roots, preventing it from growing back. Horses have both upper and lower incisors and graze by "clipping the grass," similar to a lawn mower, allowing the grass to easily grow back.

In addition, the horse's digestive system does not thoroughly degrade the vegetation it eats. As a result, it tends to "replant" its own forage with the diverse seeds that pass through its system undegraded. This unique digestive system greatly aids in the building up of the absorptive, nutrient-rich humus component of soils. This, in turn, helps the soil absorb and retain water upon which many diverse plants and animals depend. In this way, the wild horse is also of great value in reducing dry inflammable vegetation in fire-prone areas. Back in the 1950s, it was primarily out of concern over brush fires that Storey County, Nevada, passed the first wild horse protection law in the nation.

The fact that horses wander much farther from water sources than many ruminant grazers adds to their efficacy as fire preventers. This tendency to range widely throughout both steep, hilly terrain and lower, more level areas, while cattle concentrate on lower elevations, also explains why horses have a lesser impact on their environment than livestock.: when one looks at a boundary fence where horses range on one side and cattle range on the other, the horse's' side typically reveals about 30 percent more native grasses. Their nomadic grazing habits cause horses to nibble and then move to the next bunch of grass. This is why horse range is seldom denuded unless the horses' natural grazing patterns are disrupted by human interference, mostly in the form of fencing. ("Wild Horses and the Ecosystem," 2014)

Now let's talk cattle! The Center for Biological Diversity has a wealth of information regarding the ecological and economical impacts of cattle on land in America:

The ecological costs of livestock grazing exceed that of any other western land use. In the arid West, livestock grazing is the most widespread cause of species endangerment. By destroying vegetation, damaging wildlife habitats and disrupting natural processes, livestock grazing wreaks ecological havoc on riparian areas, rivers, deserts, grasslands and forests alike—causing significant harm to species and the ecosystems on which they depend.

Despite these costs, livestock grazing continues on state and federal lands throughout the arid West. Livestock grazing is promoted, protected, and subsidized by federal agencies on approximately 270 million acres of public land in the 11 western states. Federal-lands livestock grazing enjoys more than $100 million annually in direct subsidies; indirect subsidies may be three times that.

Cattle destroy native vegetation, damage soils and stream banks, and contaminate waterways with fecal waste. After decades of livestock grazing, once-lush streams and riparian forests have been reduced to flat, dry wastelands; once-rich topsoil has been turned to dust, causing soil erosion, stream sedimentation and wholesale elimination of some aquatic habitats; overgrazing of native fire-carrying grasses has starved some western forests of fire, making them overly dense and prone to unnaturally severe fires.

Keystone predators like the grizzly and Mexican gray wolf were driven extinct in southwestern ecosystems by "predator control" programs designed to protect the livestock industry. Adding insult to injury—and flying in the face of modern conservation science— the livestock industry remains the leading opponent to otherwise popular efforts to reintroduce species like the Mexican gray wolf in Arizona and New Mexico.

The federal livestock grazing program is heavily subsidized. The western livestock industry would evaporate as suddenly as fur trapping if it had to pay market rates for services it gets from the federal government. In 2015, the Center commissioned resource economists to study the costs of livestock grazing on public lands. We found that the federal lands grazing program generated $125 million *less* than what the federal government spent on the program in 2014. Further, we found that federal grazing fees are 93 percent less than fees charged for non-irrigated western private grazing land, or just $1.69 per animal per month for each cow and calf that grazes the public land. (It costs more to feed a house cat.)

Despite the extreme damage done by grazing, western federal rangelands account for less than 3 percent of all forage fed to livestock in the United States. If all livestock were removed from public lands in the West, in fact, beef prices would be unaffected. ("Grazing")

So there you have it. Unfortunately those protecting their cattle will fight tooth and nail, and create any falsehood necessary to protect their financial interests. I am saddened that it really is about money, period. The controversies around abortion rights, gun control, immigration, citizenship, and every other big heated topic at the very least have moral, ethical, and human rights implications in the argument for a desired outcome. Our poor beloved American mustangs' very existence is threatened for one reason, and that is money. Greed at its very worst is working on the extinction of yet another species.

Lets move on from cattle grazing and our wild mustangs to breeding horses. While we need some responsible breeders (or all horse breeds would be extinct in 50 years) the majority of breeders need to be educated on responsibility and ethical standards. Parameters, licensing, fees, and registration need to be established. Breeders should no longer be able to impregnate a certain number of mares, knowing full well they will cull half (and send them to the auction house) before or shortly after they foal. Backyard breeders should be held responsible for the number of lives they put on the ground as well. Many times, the mare or stallion shouldn't be reproducing for a variety of reasons. Temperament, physical conformation, and genetic history all play a role in determining whether or not to breed. But what do I hear? "It would be so fun to have a foal here!" Or, "if I can't ride her anymore, I'll breed her." Or, "there are pregnant mares ready to foal on the kill lot, HELP!" I ask you now, how is this responsible? People breed with no consideration or conscious to the bigger picture. These are living beings, with hearts and minds!

Let's move on to other atrocities.

Premarin mares: As we touched upon earlier with Dazzle and her foal, there are many wrongs in this industry and the entire industry needs to be ended, shut down, period. The production of Premarin (an estrogen based Hormone Replacement Therapy known as HRT) is derived from the urine of pregnant mares. This is abuse for each horse from start to finish. The mares are bred continually until they drop dead on the line. They are kept in cramped confined conditions for years. Their foals are sold for meat. There is zero reason for Premarin to exist. There are alternatives for those who would argue that it's a medical necessity.

Race horses: While this sport has been titled the "Sport of Kings," the horses pay the price for this entertainment. It is a well-known and accepted fact that failed and injured racehorses, whom no longer have the potential to return a profit, have very little commercial value, and are therefore mostly discarded. The majority of Thoroughbreds will meet their fate on an abattoir floor. This means a brutal ending—slaughter.

The racing industry denies this claim, emphatically proclaiming love for its animals. Yet in most cases, once a horse is deemed unprofitable it is ruthlessly discarded. I have had a conversation with a woman who's father bred Thoroughbreds...for racing. She was kind and very soft spoken as she explained how all she saw was love, respect, and the very best of care provided for his horses. It was refreshing to hear. It was like a small glimmer of hope, a small light shining on the ugly fate of horses bred for racing.

One problem is that horse racing is a self-regulated, money-driven industry. How are we to know the truth about what really happens to discarded racehorses? Go look up how many horses die on the racetrack each week. You will be shocked. Look up the story of Ferdinand, the 1986 Kentucky Derby winner. He ended up on the slaughterhouse floor. I must add that in just the past four years I have seen efforts being made to provide retirement for racehorses. How they are treated day to day while racing remains to be seen only behind barn doors. I cling to that woman's kind testimony of love and respect as my small beacon of hope.

Next up, let's address our three remaining gems that, remember, keep our horses suffering: convenience, laziness and ego.

I'm going to demonstrate the four "gems" at work. But I'd like to start with a positive and a solution. My suggestions, baby steps if you will, are provided to help create awareness for the person—and relief for the horse. I'll share some ways to resolve the human-first agenda behind each of these things that cause suffering of horses.

So, You Just Want to Ride?

A complete understanding of the physical, emotional and spiritual status of the horse should be everyone's goal especially before mounting. It could keep you safe for life while riding, not to mention honoring the horse. *This won't work, you say, it takes to long, it's not economical. I just want to rent this horse, and go for a trail ride.*

So, I pause here, keep pausing—OK—it makes sense to you to hop on a 1,000-pound animal you met 10 seconds ago and proceed to kick his sides and pull on his mouth to ride? Meanwhile you're putting your safety and trust in the stranger helping you up, the one who is profiting financially from this? Let's look at statistics from 2010. Sit down as pony and horse accident statistics make for uncomfortable reading:

- Approximately 15 million people ride a horse or pony every year in the United States.

- One in five horse related injuries occur on the ground before the horse has been mounted.

- Mounted injuries most often involve a fall and dismounted injuries most often involve kicking.

- Dismounted injuries are usually more serious than mounted injuries.

- Most riding injuries are sustained by amateurs whilst pleasure riding.

- Head injuries are the most common cause for admission to hospital and death.

- The highest rates of injury occur to those aged between 5 and 14, and 25 and 44 years.

- A rider who has one head injury has a 40 percent chance of suffering a second head injury.

- There are approximately 75,000 horse related visits made to emergency rooms by riders every year.

- The most frequent injuries include fractures, lacerations and head injuries. The most frequent cause of death is head injury.

- The most frequent cause of multiple injuries in a *sport of any description* is horse riding.

Do I have your attention now?

Precisely. Horses deserve better than being treated as objects. A solution can be as easy as a renter walking the horse prior to mounting. If they have no horse experience, then someone who can keep them safe must accompany them. Make each rider spend 10 minutes AT LEAST before any mounting. Do they even know how to ride, how about some pointers to keep horses happier? A moment connecting could keep you safe.

To do my very best by the horse means I have to get to know them as an individual. They each have their own personality, likes and dislikes, moods, and issues. They are sentient beings. If you disagree with this notion then I am excited to share the facts, testimonies and experiences from true horse whisperers. Before starting a horse under saddle, riding, doing trails, renting, owning or leasing, the first step should be getting to know the horse—on the ground. Many talented horse people suggest that numerous, hundreds of hours on the ground should take place prior to ever getting in the saddle! Some extremely talented horse people can connect, heal, and transform a horse in minutes. Most of us fall short of that accomplishment, and so we should at the very least commit to take time on the ground to get to know the horse. A connection is very important. The horse needs to know you are the herd leader, the trusted friend and an ally. If this still is a difficult notion for you to think about and you feel like it'll just never happen, let me put it in human terms for you.

You're going to the dentist and you're not sure what to expect. Once escorted to the chair your nerves begin to rise. It is at this moment the dentist arrives and says hello. Warm and friendly, she touches your shoulder and you immediately begin to breathe a little, feeling reassured you're in good hands. She explains a bit about what is about to transpire and you're now much more ready to open your mouth and have her begin her work. Imagine if she had just walked up to you and grabbed your face, opened your mouth and began sticking her hands in there! A little consideration goes a long way. Don't ever think horses don't understand. They interpret, feel, manage and understand nuance beyond our own capabilities.

If I'm lazy, I want a shortcut. If I am teaching students to ride and I don't have time! There are financial issues here for people. I know, I get it, but don't be impatient and don't be lazy! Put the horse first. Instructors can include learning about horses on the ground about saddling, grooming, and walking all prior to the riding lesson. It should be a prerequisite that any rider go through these fundamental steps before mounting. Any real evaluation takes time, but even a little consideration really matters. I ask, why aren't the riders grooming and tacking up their own mounts before a lesson? If this occurred, the horse would be given the chance to say hello to the rider, and the student could continue practicing these needed skills. But time is money in the human world. (Side note: I have seen English competitions where multiple girls mount and ride one horse through a vigorous competition. They take turns hopping on, racing over jumps, and return to throw the horse back into the "box" while the next person eagerly waits to charge out and complete the same course. This is insanity to me, not to mention an accident waiting to happen.)

CHAPTER 28

Let's Talk Language!

Let's talk about language, just for a moment. How many people do you know that call their horses, or someone else's horses, names? She's nag! He's untrainable. That horse is so stupid! How often have you heard people make horrible "female" comments when mares come into estrus? Estrus, or heat, is the period of the reproductive cycle when the mare ovulates and if bred is likely to conceive. Estrus is also the time when the mare is receptive and will accept the stallion. I will never know why this opens up an opportunity for humans to start using foul language when referring to mares during this time. "She's a whore! A hussy! A tramp!" These comments are made because she is following a natural cycle and her natural instincts. Personally, I think it's shameful. It falls into the category with all the other vulgar misuses of language people choose to use.

Cowboys, dressage riders, jumpers, rodeo people, trainers, and barn owners often come to see what horses are available for adoption. Many of them view the horse as just an animal, a riding mechanism, or a tool to be used. Of course, many horse people are unaware of the qualities we have discussed. Or even if they do acknowledge it they believe them to be unimportant. Their agenda sends them on a hunt to purchase a horse. My mind races as I stand in conversation with people. Let me show you what I mean.

I'll share what I hear and what my thoughts are about statements made by others regarding horses:

- "I need to sell my horse."
  (I need to rehome my horse)

- "How much to buy this horse?"
  (We don't sell horses. We adopt them into new homes)

- "This horse is junk."
  (This horse is not a good fit for me)

- "Is she broke to ride?"
  (We don't break things here. How about, is she well trained under saddle?)

- "This horse is un-trainable."
  (I am not qualified to train this horse)

- "I need to get rid of my horse."
  (I need to rehome my horse)

- "My horse is dangerous."
  (My horse is too much horse for me)

- "It's the horses fault."
  (It's NEVER the horse's fault.)

- "My horse is mean by nature"
  (Your horse is completely misunderstood.)

I stand and listen as I learn all about the desires of the person visiting. Sometimes, while I feel it's my opportunity to help shift the perspective ever so slightly, I will only make one suggested comment that helps get my point across. I have to be patient. Change takes time.

Many potential adopters are not a good fit for one of our horses. It would be a tragedy to raise a horse with respect and bring them up expecting to be treated in trust based partnership methodologies only to be betrayed. These are living entities, sentient beings, and our thought processes about how they're treated needs adjusting. Many people share with me that this attitude should be shared for all living creatures. While I do agree, I must remember for now, once again, we are talking about horses. So, as you can see my job is to help people see the gifts and the value of a horse. From there it begins to get easier. Some people flow right into the kindness and rapidly understand this unseen connection. Others? Well, we take it one sentence at a time.

The most used statement I hear over and over again, even by really good trainers is "broke to ride." Really? We all need to stop and acknowledge THERE IS NO NEED TO BREAK A HORSE. Partner instead! Many cultures still use this term and many still hit, brutalize, beat, sack out, damage, control, and dominate a horse as their method to starting them. It's heinous, and extremely abusive. I will provide many resources such as videos to watch and books to read that confirm my statements. Or, come visit my facility where I can show you the two things. The first is the results of years of abuse, some subtle, some horrific. The second is the miracle of rehabilitation. A partner is a much safer and happy horse.

Dominance and cruelty have no place when working with horses. If you think so then it is your (uneducated) ego. Check in and see if you are willing to learn a proven, better, way. How about "less abusive" methods of training? Don't laugh! Abuse comes in little doses and is every bit as damaging. Remember the good ol' human agenda. The items I consider abusive are used everywhere everyday: Acepromazine tranquilizers, stud chains on mares, some spurs, some use of crops, most bits, some twitches, and even headstalls. It is the people and how they use these items. I can hear the critics now.

"What have you accomplished? You're not even a trainer."

I don't need to be. My volunteers and I have been rehabilitating the mess many trainers have been creating for years.

I have taken horses in whose only option was euthanasia. One such horse was a lovely terrified mare. Handlers deemed her dangerous, discarded her, and suggested euthanasia. She landed in our care and became a nicely adjusted horse. Once her triggers were discovered, and her plan for rehabilitation was put into place, she began to thrive. She was placed and the owner checks in happy and pleased with her mare. All is well. It's a frustrating circumstance when we have done our work and placed a horse in what we assessed as a good fit. The horse leaves happy, settled, willing and ready for their new home. Then, without asking for input or recommendations, a new trainer is hired to work with the horse. We can only observe the obvious detriment to progress in the use of old school methods including coercion, punishment, force, and a general lack of partnering. It's no surprise the new authority finds said horse un-trainable, not suitable for children, and sent back to us (with new trauma)! I have to share one circumstance when one of our fillies went into a new home and a trainer was hired to "evaluate" her. His evaluation lasted about five minutes and said "she is junk, send her back." This was a filly not even 2 years old! A sweet, very savvy Mexican cowboy came out to work with her. I smiled as the two of them stepped right up and proved that trainer wrong! This little filly was asked to get to know a big blue tarp. Not only did she approach it (could be a predator you know!) she grabbed it by the teeth and rolled herself up like a burrito. I am grateful for smart horse owners who seek out the folks who have "the touch." I have a multitude of experiences disproving a lot of these so-called experts and these trainer's evaluations. It simply is NEVER the horse's fault. I have now created a list of approved trainers in my area for my adopted horses.

The following are real statements from actual self-proclaimed "trainers" about horses who have stayed with us and are now in a permanent homes or preparing for one with a bright prognosis:

- If you cannot take this horse he will be put down today.
- He/she is dangerous. This horse should not be trusted with children.
- I have been thrown for no reason and this horse is mean by nature!
- She/he is un-trainable.
- She is dull and unresponsive. She is lazy and not a good horse.

Let's Review

In the case of the mare that would've been put down that day had we not taken her, she needed two full years of restarting coupled with an abundance of patience and letting her work it out. We were fortunate enough to know her circumstance of flipping over in the crossties and breaking her tail at the poll. Hmmm, what on earth could have caused a horse to be so terrified? I'll let you decide. Two years later she needs to be ridden without a bit and is doing wonderfully in her new home. Please note in her rehabilitation, this horse was not pushed through her issues or fear. She was allowed to work it out herself, on her own timeline. The trainer kept her agenda to be that of the horse. I can't express how often just that small adjustment would create miracles instead of trauma.

The horse that was dangerous and not trustworthy around children arrived at PMR and gave birth shortly thereafter. We hardly had the opportunity to get acquainted before she went into mother mode. Eventually, after her weanling was adopted, we evaluated her. This little mare suffers from acute anxiety, as she is extremely sensitive. She was pulled from an abusive situation and carries the emotional scars from her trauma. It took a great deal of time to help get this little mare to a place of comfort and relief. We were thrilled at the wonderful progress she had made! She was ready for a home and placed, and then the bad news hit. The new owners hired a trainer for their daughter but immediately ran into trouble with the mare.

This makes perfect sense to us as you cannot teach your students to bully their horse, well, you most certainly can, but not with a positive result. I always cringe when I hear "kick, kick, now kick!" I can immediately see there is no relationship between horse and rider. There is no connection made. The horse is navigating through a series of demands, coping as best it can, going for the least amount of kicks to the side, yanks on the mouth, smacks, and pain it can endure. (Once I was asked to simply look the other way as a horrible girl smacked her horse repeatedly over the head. I walked up to her and said, "Please stop, she doesn't know what she's done wrong." Then I left the property. The woman telling me to look the other way was her trainer!)

Our sensitive little mare was returned to us with mixed stories about what had transpired. The first excuse was that many professionals deemed her un-trainable. Next it was shared that a friend has evaluated her and said she is dangerous. The last story was that the barn owner considered her un-trainable! With no offer to pay for the pick up, I went to go gather the little mare. I was happy to have her in back in an environment where she could again begin the task of walking through her new trauma. There is no amount of questions and interrogation that can guarantee the hired trainer will have any idea of how to work with horses. There is no credential or degree. Even if there was such a thing, it's unreliable. Our PMR trainer has confidence this little mare will work through her issues, and for that I am grateful.

Remember the horse throwing a person for "no reason" and mean by nature? That beautiful black gelding was hours from euthanasia. Deemed mean and nasty, I was surprised how easily he loaded for me. Once at the rescue he immediately became the sweetest boy imaginable. He was the kind of horse that would rest his muzzle on your shoulder from behind. He nuzzled your ear-lobes for fun. He is one of those horses I wish I could have kept. I think of him often and smile missing his sweet antics. Why was he deemed so dangerous you ask? His spine was out in four places and he was in acute discomfort. With six weeks of chiropractic adjust-ments and light bodywork, this gelding became transformed. Once out of pain his personality blossomed. Of course, being a stunning shade of jet black, his name was Shadow. He is now well loved in his new home.

Now, let me tell you about the story of the "un-trainable" horse. This particular horse simply needed someone who put his or her own agenda aside, and allowed her to learn at her own pace. She became a wonderful trail partner for an older woman.

Lastly, can you guess the circumstance of the "dull and unre-sponsive" horse that was deemed simply lazy? This horse is our first gal, Rose. As you know she was diagnosed with a traumatic brain injury. She is neurologically damaged, not stubborn. I thought Rose would love the extra attention and I placed her on a non-riding adoption contract that was immediately violated. She is back and in permanent sanctuary with our rescue.

These stories are testament that learning to partner and taking the time is key to making life long progress while building success-ful, unmatched relationships with equines. Not only do we build relationships, but also begin to look past the physical when resolving "undesirable" behaviors in our equine partners.

For example, horses suffering from ulcers should not be a common occurrence, yet it is. There are two possibilities here. The first is that horses are biologically designed to eat 18 hours a day and the acid in their stomach continues to work even if there is no hay there. Some horses get fed only once or twice per day. The second possible reason for high rate of ulcers is that horses physically manifest stress and the result of coping with that stress is an ulcer. It is a physiological response to the treatment they are receiving. I reiterate that if we take just the physical attributes, we may determine she is sound, has nice ground manners, or likes to jump, but the bigger questions remains. How well adjusted is she? Does she trust? What are her triggers? And, a much more critical question, is she on the edge of a nervous breakdown? For me it is these kinds of questions that are the more important factors. Discovering the answers to these questions will put us on a path for finding the very best fit possible. The answer to these types of questions cannot be discovered right away and time is the necessary ingredient.

We are interested in creating a safe and happy horse, and a great experience for an adopter. We are looking to place every horse into a home for the rest of his or her life. I have said earlier that less than 1 percent of equines have one home for life. That is a sad statistic. The rest of their lives you say? Yes, I did. It's a huge commitment. It's an important commitment. It's a life-changing commitment. I can hear the peanut gallery grumble that it sounds like a lot of work and time. I retort with don't be lazy, make the time, because our horses deserve it.

I often hear that "my child has outgrown this horse." This is an extremely common statement, and very well accepted by most the general public. The general public meaning people—not horses.

For horses it can be a huge heartbreak. I understand well that life happens. But transition is a much better solution than just being done with them. Once the owner's interest has waned, cultures find it acceptable to sell, "get-rid-of", move them along, dump them, abandon them, or even worse to leave them to starve somewhere in an empty field or pasture. This I have seen many times. Is there not a transition period available for another person to fall in love with this horse, while you shift away? How hard can that be? Rescues are all over the nation trying to create that bridge and make that help available. It is kinder to the horse.

We will often hear that people are ready for a horse that can jump higher, go faster, or any number of things. It seems it's more convenient to just move on, ignoring the emotional status of your current horse. The same comments above apply here. A transition time would be immensely helpful to the horse that one is ready to move on from.

Many times horses are rehomed because the child owner has grown and is off to college. Convenience and financial implications get in the way of what is good for the horse. I see young girls crying at the thought of giving up their horse. I imagine the horse standing in silence with a broken heart. Can't the horse be leased until she returns? Are you certain a college student's life will never return to having a horse share it with them?

What is hardest for me to digest is when I hear "our horse is getting too old and cannot do the same work." This is when our horses need us the most. They have served us, loved us and stood by us, sometimes, for many, many years and the best that humans seem to be able to do is discard them. This is acceptable in many horse communities and people feel very strongly that they are doing right by the horse. Feedlots are full of horses just over the age of "usefulness." That word again!

In 2018, I came across such a horse in its senior years that had been dumped on a lot in North Dakota. I was working with a lovely woman getting this group of equines some attention and into new homes. This old ranch horse had a note on his halter. It said, "Best roping/ranch horse I've ever owned." Why would a person leave his old horse on a lot in a North Dakota January winter knowing that he would ship to slaughter? Most of us don't do it to our cats, dogs, or even our pet rodents. It is a money-driven convenience, a usefulness-only mindset, and a "horses are a commodity" mentality behind those decisions. I find it irresponsible, outrageous and unacceptable. With the help from Pregnant Mare Rescue, Old Man Joe was pulled off the lot and put up in a warm comfy barn, thick with straw bedding. His caregiver spent the time to hand feed him grain, reassuring him all would be well. The morning found Joe had crossed over sometime in the night. RIP Joe. The world is a cruel place.

So at this time, perhaps, we can understand why in rescue that some horses arrive angry and others are withdrawn and depressed. Their vacant eyes reflect years of being mistreated, years of not knowing what a day may bring, or perhaps the sad reality of just being ignored.

My own eyes witness little girls enrolled in fancy riding programs being told to smack 'em, and kick! If they don't go, yank on those bits if they don't listen! And my trips to the feedlot have seen gorgeous well-trained horses turned in like a used car before the tires show wear.

My blood also boils regarding horses used for high-end show jumping. There are plenty of equestrians that spend a fortune on their "strand" of horses. This strand is an accumulation of the horses one individual uses in their "treasure chest" for competing. In order to win, one must hold a lot of treasure. It reminds me of a harem. Nobody is specifically recognized as an individual, you are just part of a group put to the task to service an individual who may or may not care about you. These horses often are valued in the $500,000 range. And one person will have two or three or five? I hear the argument of, "Don't you think they care about these animals…they are worth a fortune!" I respond by saying that the answer lies in taking a walk through that barn. There they stand. Look into their eyes, and you will know whether or not they are loved. If you're unable to get a firsthand glimpse, the full-length documentary "The Path of a Horse," featuring renowned trainer Stormy May, reveals some of what I am describing.

CHAPTER 29

Horses Heal

Horse riding therapy, known as Hippotherapy, has long been acknowledged and credited for providing fantastic benefits for people with physical challenges. Within the past 30 years, great strides have been made in methodologies that provide mental health benefits to clients via horses.

Created in 1989, Equine Guided Education, or EGE, has been hosting programs in leadership development, coach training, and consciousness shifting. SkyHorse EGE™ developed the concept that leadership is about relationships. They focus on developing clarity about how one relates to themselves and one's life path, how one relates to others, how one relates to our worldview, and our desires to contribute to a worthy cause.

I have taken a workshop at the SkyHorse Ranch, and the experience is nothing less than astounding. How can horses—by just being in their company—bring up such raw untapped emotion? Did you know that if you stand in the middle of a circle-shaped corral (a round-pen) and make a false statement of who you are, how you are, or more, the horse in the corral with you will ignore you? Make a true statement and they will come into the center of the circle and join you. Do they read our energy, feel our sentiment, and know better than we possibly can the emotional state of our own wellbeing? (How do you feel about slaughtering them now, eating them, or beating them?)

The EAGALA Model (Equine Assisted Growth And Learning Association) is a distinct experience-based, team approach framework designed to empower clients to better analyze their situations, make connections, and find their own solutions through personal and physical experiences. The association claims that over the past 17 years its clients have reported being able to change and grow more effectively and quickly than through traditional approaches. In summary, equestrian therapy (equine therapy or equine-assisted therapy) is a form of therapy that makes use of horses to help promote emotional growth.

When I take a moment to reflect on all the ways that horses serve us and do for us, it really drives me to want a better understanding for them. This is where better treatment will begin. I'm not sure how they do it, but they do. They never say a word, sometimes they push a little into your space, sometimes they even smell, and sometimes they ignore you completely. But that invisible healing magic is doing its work, and it happens every time.

A woman came to visit the ranch and I could see the empty sadness in the eyes of someone trying to fill the day and make it go by faster. Something had occurred that brought her much grief. We chatted a bit and I learned of her circumstance. Her husband had just passed and, still numb, I believe she thought a trip to see the horses would get her mind off her sorrow if for just an instant. The distraction would be a welcome relief.

As we strolled the grounds I invited her to come meet our new colt. Born only 24 hours earlier, he was the picture of life and joy bounding around his mother.

She smiled and became teary eyed, "He is so handsome." I said let's name him in honor of your husband. She looked at me wide eyed and in disbelief.

"Really? You would do that?"

I smiled and said I would if she promised to come visit him. Esteban received daily visits and, in no time, the two became fast friends. She learned of haltering and giving fanny scratches. He learned about kindness and love and being a good boy. As the weeks turned into months, I could see a twinkle in her eyes. They were beginning to come back to life. She was often smiling or crying, sometimes at the same time. But she was walking her path and understood this was the place to do just that.

On a sunny midweek afternoon, as Esteban was approaching 7 months of age, his pal arrived. She knew he would soon be ready for adoption. With a kiss on his nose and a hug, she looked at me and said, "Thank you. I can breathe again, and it's time for me to go." That was the last time I saw her, her last visit. Esteban was adopted into a lovely home and I believe his new family kept his name when they learned the backstory.

It was later that same year a beautiful black and white mare came to us in foal. She had been abandoned on a ranch up in northern California. I always wish I had more details and more information but I rarely get any. We never know the dads, and often not a lot about the situation. We just help the mares get to safety. We called this beautiful mare Star, and the day she foaled a woman arrived obviously grieving. Her posture at the site of this brand new colt was information enough for me. She stood hunched, forlorn as if her knees may give out any moment.

After the initial hello and taking in her stature, I figured to get right to the issue. "What has happened?" I inquired. "Is there something I can do for you?"

She had just come from putting her dog to rest and decided she didn't know where to go. She drove aimlessly. She just drove until she thought of coming out to the horses. She came straight from the veterinarian's office, to my ranch? *Oh boy*, I thought. *I'm not much of a counselor. Horses don't use words. I am much better with the wordless kind of conversation.* She was enormously emotional and trying to just keep it together.

"Tell me about him," I said as we walked.

She began to breathe again. *OK, this is good,* I thought, *breathing is important.* Her beloved shepherd Maverick had been losing traction in his hind hip area and the time from diagnosis to death was just too fast. She was still trying to wrap her head around the thought that he was sick when he already needed to cross over. We stood shoulder to shoulder at the paddock looking at this beautiful new life and once again I found myself suggesting to name a newborn after a departed loved one. She burst into tears and hugged me with the strength of a lumberjack.

Maverick became the center of her world, enjoying daily visits and attention. He was quite a handful and often needed intervention from myself or another ranch hand when he became obstreperous! No matter, she delighted in every antic and every tantrum he displayed. I could feel that simply honoring her lost love was healing and helping her move forward. Again when the time approached to wean Maverick from momma, my visitor was ready to go find her own new love. I could see the gratitude in her expression she said goodbye and thanked me. I silently smiled and thought, *don't thank, me it's those amazing horses.*

I have wanted to share for some time the healing that I witness here at the ranch. The loss of someone you love is incapacitating, overwhelming. It doesn't matter if they were human, an animal, or if the crossing was imminent. The pain, the loss, and grief are real.

One of the amazing gifts I have been privileged to observe is the gift of walking the path from paralyzing grief to the glimmer of light, a possibility of coping. These animals are simply light workers, bringers of hope and calm. It is miraculous to me the work they accomplish without ever uttering a single word.

The visitors come. They come to enjoy the peace here, and to be in the presence of these large warmhearted beasts. Where else can you go and be welcomed in the company of horses? Where else can you go inside the paddock of a mare and a week-old foal to experience such precious moments? If you don't own your own horse, or have money to go learn to ride, it's difficult to find a welcoming situation.

I love that the kids come out to visit. Some of them have challenges but the horses pay no mind to such differences. It is unimportant and they pay no attention. They lower their heads and stand quietly while they are brushed and adored. The excitement can be difficult to contain. I had a 3-year-old child stand close to our newest filly. She was a preemie and at 3 weeks of age she was still tiny. His little hand was on her neck and they gazed at one another.

"Mom?" was all he said as he grinned in astonishment.

I smiled. That was all that was needed. Magic is like that.

This little filly was named Nutmeg and we called her momma Arianna. "Ari" was relinquished to us thin and crusty looking, and with her dull coat we couldn't even tell she was a beautiful roan. This is the image of the undernourished. She needed groceries and supplements. While the vet guesstimated that she would foal in about three months, this mare had other plans. Less than three weeks into her stay I found her little filly newborn in the shavings at about 8 a.m. I stood watching and immediately noticed baby was having trouble standing. The placenta was at the opposite end of the foaling stall so some movement must have occurred. I watched a moment more and realized this baby couldn't stand at all. I entered the stall and reassured mom that all was well. I leaned into the little thing and helped her up. The wobbly legs began flailing in all directions. She backed up and found herself sort of leaning against my lap but standing. I crouched in my half-flexed squatting position and began to take inventory. I was looking for deformities in the hoof and leg structure. Where was her shoulder and spine? All seemed to be in the right places and I summarized that she was put together properly. Dr. Natalie would confirm my thoughts.

Mom approached with a soft nicker and baby began to nurse. I remained still, positioned to provide the necessary stability for the little girl. This began the next 24 hours of close watching. I checked every two hours all afternoon. She was nursing eagerly but still having trouble standing. I prepared mentally for the long night ahead.

Flashlight in hand, my visits were warmly welcomed as I silently congratulated myself on my isometrics! The little girl learned quickly and was prepared to eat immediately. By dawn I was exhausted, but baby was warm and well fed. It was getting late in the afternoon and I was getting ready to go help feed when my good news arrived! I witnessed little Nutmeg getting herself up and over to mom! Oh, thank goodness. I went to go nap.

After consulting with the Steinbeck Equine Hospital it was decided that we would haul them both down to the facility for evaluation. The vet examined both and found that Ari had sustained significant injuries in the birthing process. This young mare, barely 3 years old, was torn up. On a happy note, the doctors fussed over the foal, enjoying a "healthy " baby.

"We don't get to see healthy foals," one doctor spoke as she stroked Nutmeg's neck. "It's so fun to see the new life."

I noted that Nutmeg was a mere 48 hours old! With doctor's orders, Ari and Nutmeg were sent home to heal. Shredded flesh can't be stitched up and reconstruction cannot take place until there is tissue to work with. Antibiotics and painkillers were prescribed to help Ari get through the next few weeks. Day after day I found this mare was laying flat out in her stall snoring. Exhaustion had set in. Over the next two months, while Ari recuperated, Nutmeg gained strength and coordination. She was still petite but thriving.

That special feeling of a new foal had the children giddy with excitement. The warm weather was here and my ranch was the favorite place to be for the children. They collected their pennies to donate to our "Pennies for PMR" program. Anxious and very serious, they arrived to choose the horse that their hard-earned donation would help!

It was that same spring I had met a young man via social media claiming to be new to the area and looking for work. He claimed to be a farrier and said he was great, a natural with horses. His profile on Facebook showed he and his pals riding bareback in halters, smiles all around. Gus wanted to come and trim hooves. He was friendly, in his mid-20s, and as a farrier new to the area who was enthusiastic about working. I invited him out to meet the horses. He strolled around and immediately fell for, you guessed it, our gorgeous roan Ari. Her little filly Nutty stuck her nose up to the paddock rail checking out the visitor.

"How much? Can I buy her? I'll take her today."

With furrowed brows I responded with tentative energy, "We don't *sell* horses here. We are a rescue. You don't know a thing about this horse."

My thoughts began to run. *You are here to trim, I didn't realize you were in the market for a horse. What would be your plan for a horse? Ah, can you see she is still nursing a baby?*

Gus proceeded to tell me he likes the Mexican rodeos and he would "break her" to rope or rein Over my dead body I struggled with how I could share my wealth of information and opinions about "breaking" a horse.

"We don't break horses, we start them. We don't particularly endorse the Mexican Rodeo lifestyle for a horse."

Trying to respectfully explain the subtle differences in cultures left Gus annoyed and confused.

He said, "Well then, let me trim her feet for you, I want to get my hands on her."

My mother bear instincts were in full gear by now. I stated that this mare is learning about picking up her feet as she is not ready for a trim just yet."

"No problem," says Gus. "I'll just put a snaffle in her mouth and work her a bit, she'll come around."

By now I am practically escorting this young man off the property. His response demonstrated a complete lack of horse skill and knowledge. This young man has no understanding of building relationship or trust. His agenda is about taking control and working a horse until it learns to quit, to give the human what it wants. How many people do you know that think this is fine? It is not fine, not if you're building trust. This is an extremely dangerous agenda as learned helplessness can be a time bomb in horses. This is a subtle example but very accurate nonetheless. This particular mare was given a full six months while she nursed her filly to learn to pick up her feet for a trim. She also learned to trust us and that she is safe and respected here. She is a willing, confident, well-adjusted mare and, even though she is a rescue, she will make someone a fine horse. Our approach has created a partnership that is teaching this mare about coming into situations from a completely different perspective than a horse that is bullied. Ari will never need sedation to be trimmed as she was given the chance to learn.

My rescue has been criticized for our training methods. I have heard it said that we let them do whatever they want. Suggestions have been made that we better get training, which suggests we are not training, or that allowing daily liberty is somehow irresponsible. Our response is to quietly go our own way. There are well-known, respected, and even world famous trainers that employ the same philosophies and methods. And their results are fantastic.

CHAPTER 30

Reflections On Rescue
As It Relates To My Life

As I reflect on all the sad and unbelievable ways the world has come to interact with horses, it brings to my mind another situation near to my heart. As I work in rescue, I also divide my time helping my elderly parents. I observe similarities—disturbing similarities. We often dole out the same horrible treatment to our elderly. I am not surprised, but I am saddened. I ask, what is wrong with being old? Why do we shove our elders to the side? It's just like our horses. The perception is that they both are no longer useful.

Imagine how many stories and how many life experiences someone who has lived 80 or 90 years must hold. I remember when I would visit my Grandfather. I was a little girl and I would sit on the floor next to his chair. He would talk about coming over from Italy when he was a teenager. He was 15 years old when he came to America alone. He experienced Ellis Island and traveled from New York clear across the country to Washington State. When I asked what year he was born he would smile and place the palm of his hand upon my head.

"1888."

I couldn't even comprehend that long ago.

Gifts, whether from a patient, older horse or a wise grandfather, can be subtle and sometimes initially hidden. I feel it is a shame when they slip through our hands.

So, how does one facilitate change? I am a realist. I appreciate that circumstances do occur which alter what we can afford to provide. As we say, shit does happen. But I believe the underlying problem is bigger than money or current events. It's attitude. Change lies within the attitude. So I have to ask, can we ALL work on this, *for the love of horse?*

I have read and been told that there are three stories to any incident or disagreement: your story, their story and the true story. Yes, one side may be the same as another, but all three exist. In my mind and now in my heart, I can see the truth in this and the gift of understanding it has given me. This understanding creates a sort of peace and acceptance. Making peace with one's demons paves the road for healing and the elimination of creating an environment for disease. A lot of my frustration and inner turbulence has started to settle.

I have learned that because these life situations carry more than one story, it is useful for me to create percentages. For example, it is a habit of mine to try and find something to like or appreciate about everyone I can. Well, sometimes it's only 10 percent. Yes, the rest of their personality, their moral (or immoral) compass, general attitude, views, politics (you get the picture) doesn't resonate with me. Creating a percentage has helped me acknowledge the differences that exist in relationships and create perspective. I don't have to bury these differences inside or stuff them away any longer. Instead, I can prepare mentally to take care of myself. It has become a tool for me to control my emotional status and protect my well-being. The upside to this habit is I never have to like every-thing about anyone again. This is a great tool for me as I was raised to keep everybody happy, make peace and be liked. It's freedom from a continued self-created obligation.

Life is such a mixed bag. It is heartbreaking and joyful, diffi-cult and then easy, simple and, of course, so complex. It was in the following year that I felt the weight of my responsibility to the horses and to those I love full force. It was so powerful and over-whelming I could have dropped physically to my knees. These lives are important and before me lies such a large, daunting, seeming impossible task, yet it is as necessary and as hopeful as the very next breath I will take. But what I couldn't know is as committed and passionate I was about this project, I was about to be knocked to my knees.

CHAPTER 31

Take The Bad With The Good.

I remember the time vividly, and I am horrible at timelines from the past. But my beautiful niece was getting married on Saturday and it was the Friday before, at precisely 4:36 p.m., in which my news was delivered to me. The irony of such bad news in the midst of such a joyous occasion was absurd to me. My entire family would be asking about it tomorrow in confidence, in a hush-hush tone, at a wedding, a time of such special happiness. I was searching internally for options. How many times would I have to say it?

"Yes, the results came back, I have breast cancer."

I was diagnosed in July of 2015. I felt that the timing was hideous and I even thought of just telling a fat lie about it a moment's consideration. But of course that was out of the question.

Yet, those words can stop you in your tracks. The emotional storm that began to brew internally for me was unprecedented. I was raging and crying and standing perfectly still all in the same moment. I barely got through the Saturday wedding. Dave and I were gratefully seated with the bride's neighbors and distant in-laws, people who didn't need to know much. I found myself withdrawing from people and company. Socialization became extremely painful for me because I wanted to tell everyone I have cancer. I wanted to scream to anyone who would listen that I was afraid I might die. Odd, I know. Unacceptable? You bet. Most people keep it to themselves. They are brave in the face of death—stoic and strong. I wasn't any of those things. I was pissed off and frustrated and feeling terrified. Everything and everyone bothered me. I would scold myself, *For Heaven sakes Lynn, children deal with this monster better.* I lashed out at neighbors, relatives, siblings, and even my own children. I didn't realize I was in the midst of a nervous breakdown.

Every hospital visit, every test and consultation, I usually went to alone. Jillian was the only soul I allowed in. I cocooned myself and shut out the world. I wouldn't make eye contact unless absolutely necessary, as in when I had to check into a doctor's appointment. I would barely look up, mumble and go take my seat. I have never felt so isolated in my life. But it was all I could do. I wasn't responding appropriately to this diagnosis. I was feeling ashamed. I was not anybody's hero, or anybody you would look up to. I was feeling very small. I was pitiful and full of self-hatred.

Friends and family would send me letters, Get Well cards, and I only felt undeserving. I wanted to scream, "I am **not** the bravest person you know! It is not guaranteed that I'm going to be fine. I may be dead. I'm not ready to be dead. I am not ready for any of this. I don't want any of this. Can't it just go away?"

I made the decision to have both breasts chopped off. They have a nice term for it: Bi-lateral mastectomy. And I took the next step and opted for reconstructive surgery right then and there. They would pull tissue from my abdomen and create fake breasts. I was so interested in getting it all over with at once and being done, that I just leapt. I jumped into the dark and frightening abyss of the unknown.

When the morning of my surgery arrived, Dave and I drove quietly in the dark. Arriving at the hospital before sunrise was my preference. No people, no traffic, no noise. I signed in and sat down next to my beloved husband. Dave held my hand and tried to comfort me. I'm not certain I was even present as I can't remember one word spoken.

The time to go to my room and prep had arrived. I was escorted down the hallway into my room. Dave fumbled around with the overnight bag trying to hide his nerves, but I know him too well. I felt badly for his worry. I thought, *you sweet man, there is absolutely nothing anyone can do now. Worry can't change a thing.* I thought of my daughter, my son. I looked into Dave's eyes and thought the next 12 hours would be difficult.

The time had arrived and the lingering darkness outside painted the mood. I slipped into my little gown and struggled to admit I was finished undressing. That meant I was ready to move. I was escorted down the hall of the hospital corridor in my green gown. I was barefoot thinking how odd to be walking. I was asking myself, *don't I get some kind of drowsy drug so that I don't care about any of this?* I thought they put you on a table and rolled you down the hall. Then all you have to do is look at the ceiling. No faces or expressions to have to deal with, and certainly no smiles.

The doctor was on my left and Dave was on my right, squeezing my hand. We paused at the exit door. I leaned in and kissed my husband while barely making eye contact. It was too hard because all my thoughts flooded forth…*Will I see you again? Is this it? Am I really doing this?* I stood quietly and watched him push open the double doors. He was gone. It was such a strange feeling watching him walk through those doors. I felt myself running, wanting to catch up, but there I stood and then the hand of a stranger was holding mine. Not bothering to acknowledge my doctor's company I looked forward and began to walk toward the double swinging doors at the end of the hallway. Surgery was posted above the door.

The doctor cautioned me about climbing onto the table and helped as I maneuvered up. It was cold and I appreciated the thin veil of my gown between the table and my skin. Of course I had never seen a true operating table. It was odd looking, the color of metal with a small indent right in the middle. Strangely I remember thinking it looked like a large meat tray. The kind of tray one might see behind the butcher counter. The kind one might see in a slaughterhouse. The indent must exist so liquids flow to center and not to the floor. I was still adjusting as my eyes took in the room. This was a mistake.

There stood two long tables making a right angle toward me. Covered in green tablecloths, I noted they matched my gown. There were instruments for surgery, metal heavy looking objects taking up every inch of the tabletop. Saws, drills, clamps. I quickly chose to lie down. I was looking for the ceiling again.

Big glaring lights and the feel of motion surrounded me but I was done observing and chose to lie still. It was then a muzzle appeared and took up every inch of my view. The whiskers disappeared into my face as if there wasn't enough room for a muzzle and whisker hairs to fit in the allowed space above my mouth. I couldn't feel a thing. I just saw nostrils flaring, seemingly blowing air softly into mine. Huge breaths of air pushing into my nose and soft looking lips nuzzled around my face, but still I felt nothing. The smell of horse became present and I knew I was no longer alone. Struggling to make sense of what was before me I found I simply couldn't do it. I couldn't see anything but horse lips and the whiskers disappearing into my checks.

We are here and we are present. You are safe and you are loved. We are here to protect and guide. There will be no crossing today.

I was stunned. Dazzle, please Dazzle stay. I was flooded with relief. The face of what must have been the anesthesiologist broke through my vision.

"Lynn, count backward for me starting with ten."

"Ten."

Eleven hours later I opened my eyes. Nurses were efficiently bustling around, friendly, warm and kind. Their smiles were now comforting. I had survived. I spotted a painting hanging across the room. I watched as it became a puddle of liquid and slid down the wall. The colors smeared and flowed to the floor. My son sat in the chair softly gazing at me. My heart was warm as I looked on this familiar face.

"Hi, Mom. Dad's on his way." I saw my white puppy romping across the floor. What the …?

"Did you bring Merle?"

Robert smiled, "I think your hallucinating."

My bed began to rock as though I was adrift on the sea. I felt nauseous. A nurse popped in and added something to my IV. I noticed I was hooked up, and had six lines of something coming out of my body. *Drains?* Oh, I thought, OK. They look like little space capsules. I was told they were drains collecting fluid and that I had two in each breast and one coming out of each side of my abdomen. A quick smile at Robert and I drifted back to sleep.

CHAPTER 32

Recuperate In, Ahem ... Peace?

A frantic phone call came in and I reached to answer it. Looking out from a rented hospital bed to my beautiful valley view I recognized the voice of a volunteer from about 10 years before.

"Hello. Yes, well I'm recovering from surgery."

I was listening to the plea in her voice and beginning to feel badly but I was in no position to help. She was in need of a temporary place to stay. She had lost her housing and was just checking in to see if maybe I had room. It was not possible—even if there was room, even if I was up and around—as she has a cat that would immediately prevent my husband from breathing and a dog. Last thing we were in need of was another dog in the house!

I resumed my focus on healing and resting, creating a healing space with peace and serenity. Jillian had come into town to provide me with much needed assistance. Ah, the joy of washing my hair! The little tasks were undoable, unmanageable for a time. I was so thankful for my sweet daughter.

Again the call came and this time Karen was more desperate than before. I again held my ground knowing it simply was not possible. I promised to devote time to see if I could help locate a place for her. I spent hours in the rented bed gazing out my window asking for insight and divine guidance. I made phone calls for her, but they all were unproductive. There was no housing to be located. I consulted with Dave and we both reaffirmed it was not possible. The cat, the extra dog, the commotion was too much at this time. Even though Jillian was getting ready to return to school, it wasn't possible to have a boarder in our home. I once again tried to make peace and rest.

The third and fourth phone call arrived and her tone was absolutely frantic.

"I'll be under a bridge, Lynn. Please I'll camp in your backyard by the horses…*please??*"

My heart was so heavy, and I felt terrible trying to say no once again. I buckled and told her I would ask Dave if a week was possible.

Karen arrived along with her brood and began setting up digs in my daughter's bedroom on the upstairs level. It wasn't a fancy room but it was clean and comfortable. The beige carpet was worn, guilty of a few puppy accidents. The walls displayed mistakes in our painting and revealed numerous colors over the years. Jillian and I had redecorated from beige to burgundy to celery and tan tones. It was now soothing and Zen for a young adult coming home from college for visits. The bed was the most comfortable in the house. Secretly it was my retreat when I would relish staying up late reading a book I couldn't put down, or in need of an overnight snuggle with my dog. So, for now, the room was hers. The white transparent curtains floated as the breeze blew in on most afternoons. I took a last glance and closed the door.

Ten years earlier, Karen had proved her self an accomplished horsewoman and productive wonderful volunteer. She grew up in the nearby upscale equestrian community near Palo Alto, California. Woodside was a piece of paradise located in the hills above Stanford University. Her week turned into a month, and her month turned into three more months. The surprises along the way were heartbreaking.

The bottles were lined up on the kitchen table. Our bottle of Tequila, a gift from one of Dave's coworkers, was followed by a custom labeled bottle of wine. It was a wedding present from friends commemorating their special day. Beside the wine was a vodka bottle and then brandy. On our honeymoon so many years earlier we had brought back a bottle of rum from the island of St. Lucia. We had chuckled as the bottle had only a white thin label with black simple text across the front stating "100% rum." This was now empty too. With tears and apologies, Karen enrolled in a recovery program for alcoholism. I was now caring for her animals and still sitting in a hospital bed.

I am naïve in the ways of abuse. The habits and manipulative manner in which addicts run their lives was very foreign to me indeed. The months did pass and while horse care and horse help remained productive, there was an evil addiction taking place right under our noses. Dave and I were blind and vulnerable. We believed the lies, and the half-truths. We were completely unaware that a much bigger monster was living right under our roof. If alcohol is an evil addiction, heroin is the devil himself.

Chugging up the driveway I vaguely glanced at Karen's little white truck sitting in its designated parking spot. I pulled into the back area surveying the pastures and paddocks. Strolling past the hay shed I chatted with my barn manager a moment and understood Karen was not with the horses. Unconcerned I headed to the house.

The sweet smile of my husband was the usual welcome.

"Where's Karen?" I inquired. "Upstairs?"

"Haven't seen her," Dave rifled through the days mail. "I don't think she's home yet."

"I saw her car parked but she's not with the horses." I thought to myself perhaps I had just missed her, and so I headed down to her truck.

Her body was crumpled forward and leaning left, partially spilling out of the driver's door. Her right arm, caught on the steering wheel, had prevented her from hitting the asphalt. The site of her halfway hanging out of the driver's seat was startling.

"Oh my dear God, no!"

I grabbed her wrist. No pulse. I pressed my fingers to her throat. Nothing. What the hell do I know? I could be doing it wrong! I ran back to the house to grab Dave.

"Come quick! I think she's dead!"

"Oh my God!"

We bolted out of the door and down the driveway to the unforgettable site.

"What do we do?" I pulled out my cell phone and dialed 911.

"See if you can find a pulse! Get her out of the car!"

Dave's eyes welled up with tears.

"Lynn, she's gone. She's been gone a bit. Feel her skin."

I couldn't. I was frantically answering questions from the operator and getting instructions on what to do next. Before we hung up, the paramedics had arrived. For 45 minutes they worked and tried to revive her. I sent Dave up to the house as his emotions were shredded. I stood motionless as I watched the methodical actions taken in trying to save a life. The Sheriff escorted me up to the house knowing I didn't need to see the body bag. Her purse belongings revealed a spoon, a lighter, heroin, and hundreds of dollars in cash.

"We have a bad batch in the county right now," he stated quietly. "We have seen many overdoses of lately. Sometimes it's meth, sometimes crack cocaine and sometimes heroin. Right now it's heroin. Mind if we look in her bedroom?"

He spent another moment and began asking about next of kin and asking for contact information.

The door was opened and I stopped and stared. I was silenced. *Oh my God what has she done?* It was recommended that I stay out as needles can be hidden in the carpet. The empty vodka bottles were spilling out from under the bed. From the bed, the beautiful comfortable bed that was now disheveled and unkempt, the cat stared at the intruders. Dirty clothes piled up to the windowsills and filled each of the four corners. A filthy litter box overflowed with feces and kitty litter next to the closet door. No amount of breeze wafting in through the billowy curtains could contain the odor. The closet door had become her palette and the beautiful celery-colored wall had marker pen drawings of flowers and leaves. I didn't move. My eyes took in the horrific scene and I noticed some of my missing belongings strewn about the floor. Anger, yes. Frustration? Oh yes, but mostly sadness. I was overwhelmed with the sorrow of how great a loss of life is. Death is so inexplicably final. As days roll by the new memories stop, the new experiences stop, and that person becomes a thought—just a fading memory frozen in time. It seems no matter how hard one tries to make an effort to include them in the present, it falls short like a bad and insulting joke. Gone is gone from this plain.

The days continued to come: sunrise, sunset, bed, sleep, and sometimes the bad dreams. I suppose I was working through my anger, sadness, disappointment, and loss. I liked Karen. I liked her a lot. She had once had a great life as a veterinary technician and I couldn't help feel that the losses in her life over the years accumulated to more than she could get through. I was so sad.

What helps? I take time to thank God/Universe/Spirit for every blessing, and for every day. I remind myself to be patient and always be kind. Being kind can be hard! But I have to say, at the end of the day, having expressed kindness feels much better than anything else. I reach back to my percentages and smile as I continue to use those handy tools. I also live by the hard and fast rule that what you put out you will indeed get back.

I have met scores of wonderful people lifting my sites and my inspirations. I have my own personal horse faerie, Denna! Without her love and care for our equines on a daily basis this little organization would not be able to stand. She is the physical manifestation of someone understanding horses better than anyone I've met. She gets them, understands their trauma, loves them, and teaches them how to heal. It takes a community of passion, love, support, hard work, integrity, and strength. It's so hard to see the abuse. There are indeed good people in the world.

I am a blessed survivor. But the experience created an appreciation for living that I believe only "the risk of losing it all" can create. The rescue has survived recession, drought, fire, torrential rains, my own illness, and financial hardships along the way. The journey to getting it right, to healing and to providing a path for others is only the beginning and because of this I feel very small. Big task, little person.

So, moving in love and with hope, I will take one foot and place it in front of the other I will lift my head up and look forward to each morning sun and each new day. Each horror witnessed and each rude encounter expressing a different opinion is looked at as opportunity because it is the smallest effort, the smallest respectful action that will make the beginnings of a new way. It must be felt and lived each day. The action and desire for a more authentic way of living must be sought.

Social media has recently brought joyous images of friendships between the most unlikely animals. This is no accident. It is a message of hope for those listening—small messages to us all. See and be the difference. The future of our horses and our relationships not only lies within those steps but so does the very survival of our Mother Earth.

It has been an exceptional journey. I am hopeful as I bear witness to the love and commitment people have displayed over the years. This indeed keeps my ever-optimistic heart in forward motion. We are making a difference and it feels very right. We are committed to getting the word out and helping people understand. Our horses love and appreciate every single act of kindness and they deserve our very best. It is only with continued love and education that we will see our dream achieved of all horses being cared for and respected.

So I request once more, can we ALL work on this *for the love of horse?*

END

ARTICLES AND RESOURCES

Alchin, Linda. "Warhorse." *Medieval Squires*, 2018, www.medieval-life-and-times.info/medieval-weapons/warhorse.htm.

Battuello, Patrick. "Horseracing Wrongs." *Horseracing Wrongs*, 2018, horseracingwrongs.com/.

Hanes, Richard C, and Laurie Collier Hillstrom. "Paiutes." *Countries and Their Cultures*, 2007, www.everyculture.com/multi/Le-Pa/Paiutes.html#ixzz5Owh5kJtm.

"Horse Tripping Fact Sheet." *Horse Fund*, The Horse Fund, horsefund.org/horse-tripping-fact-sheet.php.

Jablonski, Virginia. "Heart of the Horse." Heart of the Horse, 2018, heartofthehorse.us/.

Parelli. "The Official Home of Parelli Natural Horsemanship - Horse Training." Parelli Horse Training, 2018, www.parelli.com/.

Paulick, Ray. "Death of a Derby Winner: Slaughterhouse Likely Fate for Ferdinand." *BloodHorse.com*, BloodHorse, 2003, www.bloodhorse.com/horse-racing/articles/180859/death-of-a-derby-winner-slaughterhouse-likely-fate-for-ferdinand.

"Shaping Civilizations: The Role of the Horse in Human Societies." *Learning Center | Equine Heritage Institute*, 2013, www.equineheritageinstitute.org/shaping-civilizations-the-role-of-the-horse-in-human-societies/.

"What Really Makes a Medicine Hat Horse?" PonyBox.com, 4 Aug. 2010, www.ponybox.com/news_details.php?id=1126.

"Wild Horses and the Ecosystem." *American Wild Horse Campaign*, 18 Dec. 2014, americanwildhorsecampaign.org/wild-horses-and-ecosystem.

www.biologicaldiversity.org/programs/public_lands/grazing/.

FURTHER READING/MATERIAL

Love This Horse, Equine Rescue Inc. www.facebook.com/lovethishorse/posts/567283236980462.

Camp, Joe. *The Soul of a Horse: Life Lessons from the Herd*. Thorndike Press, 2009.

"Free Riding USA Tour." *Free Riding NZ*, www.freeridingnz.com/.

"The Official Home of Parelli Natural Horsemanship - Horse Training." *Parelli Horse Training*, www.parelli.com/.

Hempfling, Klaus Ferdinand. All Readings and Videos.

"Homepage." *Tom Dorrance*, tomdorrance.com/about-tom/.

May, Stormy, director. *The Path of the Horse*. The Path of the Horse, www.thepathofthehorse.com/.

Nevzorov, Aleksandr. *The Horse Crucified and Risen*. Nevzorov Haute Ecole, 2011.

Pignon Frédéric, et al. *Gallop to Freedom: Training Horses with Our Six Golden Principles*. Trafalgar Square, 2015.

Rashid, Mark. *Horses Never Lie: The Heart of Passive Leadership*. Skyhorse Publishing Company, Incorporated, 2015.

"Reach Out to Horses-Horsemanship, Animal Communication, Energy Healing." *Reach Out to Horses-Horsemanship, Animal Communication, Energy Healing*, www.reachouttohorses.com/.

Resnick, Carolyn. *Naked Liberty*. Amigo Publications, Inc., 2005. https://carolynresnick.com

Heney, Elaine. *Listening To The Horse* https://listeningtothehorse.teachable.com/p/listening-to-the-horse